War Fish

by **George Grider**

as told to **Lydel Sims**

War Fish

Little, Brown and Company
Boston · Toronto

Third Printing

Published simultaneously in Canada
by Little, Brown & Company (Canada) Limited

PRINTED IN THE UNITED STATES OF AMERICA

Contents

11153

For Ann and Gayle

War Fish

I

The Silent Service

WE ALL KNEW, as 1941 lengthened, that war was coming. But the knowledge was on the surface of our minds. Subconsciously, even among those of us in the service, we rejected the idea. It was like death, I suppose: we all know we are going to die, but until we face it, until the moment actually arrives, we can't accept it.

A group of us were playing bridge at my house in San Diego the night of December 6. Someone asked me when I thought we would get into the war. "Tomorrow," I said jokingly, my partner opened the bidding with a no-trump, and the subject was dropped.

The next day Ann and our small son Billy and I were enjoying a quiet Sunday at home when a neighbor dashed in, wild-eyed, and told us Pearl Harbor had been bombed. It was weeks before I shook off the feeling that, through my flippant prediction, I had been somehow responsible.

I immediately got into my car, bade my wife and child what I felt sure was a last, fond farewell, and drove down to the division of four old S-boats to which I was attached.

They were obsolete boats, of a vintage shortly after World War I, but on that memorable day none of us doubted that we would take them immediately into combat.

One of the things I remember best about that day was the sight of a fellow officer on a nearby S-boat. He had been out on a party the night before, and when I arrived he was standing on deck, or rather hanging over the side, as sick as anybody I ever saw in my life. Minor scenes like this often burn themselves into your memory in a time of great excitement, but there is another reason I recall this one so well. Almost four years later, on V-J Day, I saw the same officer, by then the commander of his own sub, hanging over *its* side at Pearl Harbor, again violently ill. It was as fine a bit of dramatic unity as I encountered throughout the war. This, I thought, is where I came in.

Originally, I had got into submarines as I had got into the Navy, largely by chance. I entered the Naval Academy because my brother had, and he went because Charlie Brooks, a friend of ours back in Memphis, had gone, and Charlie went because he had seen a movie about Annapolis. Sons of officers killed in World War I were given a certain number of appointments every year, and the quota was never filled. So while our friends sweated and buttered up the politicians in hopes of appointments, John and I simply used the name of our father, McGavock Grider, and got our papers. I failed the entrance examination the first time, but the next year I went to a prep school in the town of Annapolis for a few months, took the examination again and passed it, and entered the Academy in 1932 just after my brother had graduated.

At first I wanted to be an aviator like my father, so much so that I used to take private flying lessons when I was home in Memphis on leave from the Academy. I still cherish a clipping of an old newspaper story in which William Faulkner, who had been a friend of my father's, wrote about Mac Grider's boy learning to fly. Later, after I got into the fleet as a catapult officer on the battleship U.S.S. *Mississippi*, I rode often with the aviators in the old seaplanes we carried and spent my meager pay on private flying.

Then, somehow, the magic wore off and I gradually decided my future was not in the air. The last time I soloed, until after the war, was one day at Pearl Harbor in 1938, shortly before Ann came out for our second wedding.

We had been married secretly just after I graduated, in violation of regulations, and now that I had served the required two years we were going to repeat the ceremony in style. I had lost my pilot's license and gone through all the red tape and delay involved in getting a duplicate. When I got it I went out and rented a little biplane for a half-hour flight in celebration of my wife's impending arrival. Within minutes after I took off, my newly acquired duplicate license blew out of my pocket, fluttered through the air, and landed somewhere in the middle of a vast sugar-cane field below me. I said the hell with flying.

After my time on the *Mississippi*, I had been ordered to the destroyer *Rathburn*. We worked with submarines in an interesting and exciting new development whereby the Navy hoped someday to be able to detect submerged boats by echo ranging — the first Navy experiments with sonar. The work was fascinating, and the life of the submarine men themselves fascinated me even more. I rode with them when I could, and soon I decided that was the life for me: small, happy ships with wonderful morale, wonderful spirit, and wonderful pay. I sent in my application and got my orders to Submarine School on May 23, 1939, the same day the *Squalus* sank during a test dive off Portsmouth, New Hampshire. I had six months' intensive training at the sub school in New London, Connecticut, and more than a year on the submarine *Skipjack* before joining the Fleet Sonar School at San Diego to teach an antisubmarine class for destroyer men. It was quite natural then that as we hurried down to our S-boats on Pearl Harbor Day, I was painfully aware of what an enemy destroyer could do to them.

We stayed in port that night, listening to the terrible tales and rumors on the radio, and the next day we set out on a war patrol. At least, it was called a war patrol, and in many ways it was. Certainly it came close to being one of the most dangerous patrols I ever made, though the danger came not from the enemy but from our own nervous actions. If we had any orders, I never knew what they were, and if we had sighted anything afloat, friend or foe, I am sure we would have tried to sink it first and identify it later. We stayed out about ten days, in a scouting line fifty to a hundred miles off San Diego, "guarding" the harbor and trying to grasp the incredible import of the war news on the radio. We were especially staggered by the news that Japanese planes had sunk the *Repulse* and the *Prince of Wales*. Until then, many of us had never really believed that planes could sink big warships.

We did finally sight one ship, and tried to make an approach on it, but fortunately it got away. I am sure now it was a friendly American tanker. It never knew what a close call it had.

Throughout the war years that followed, as combat patrols became routine and the submarine developed into one of the most effective weapons in our nation's arsenal, I never forgot the nightmare quality of that first patrol. In our ancient S-boats, uncertain of our mission and far from the heart of the conflict, we had no conception of the way of life that lay ahead of us, or of the deadly role our submarines would play in the conflict with Japan.

But the drama was already unfolding in the Pacific. During the Pearl Harbor attack itself, deck-gun crews of the submarines *Tautog* and *Narwhal* shared credit with a destroyer for shooting down one of the attacking Japanese planes. A few hours later, a bombardment of Midway by Japanese warships was broken off because of the appearance of the *Argonaut* within attack range of the enemy. It was only three days after Pearl Harbor that an enemy warship off Wake was damaged by the *Triton* in the war's first torpedo attack by a Pacific Fleet submarine. And the *Swordfish* sank a large freighter only eight days after the· attack on Pearl — the first confirmed sinking of a Japanese ship by a United States submarine. Thus, even before we returned from our excited defense of San Diego harbor, our subs in the Pacific had begun their grim mission: the torpedoing of enemy tonnage, merchant and naval alike, whenever and wherever it might be found.

The results, as the war wore on, were impressive. Plagued

at first by faulty torpedoes, limited by inadequate equipment, and forced to work out their own techniques in a form of warfare new to America, our submariners soon found their stride. The toll of enemy tonnage rose steadily through 1942 and 1943, reached a prodigious peak late in 1944, and tapered off in the closing months of the war simply because of the rapidly dwindling size of the Japanese naval and merchant marine. But the sinkings continued until the very end. The Japanese submarine *I-373*, last major naval vessel to be sunk, was downed by the *Spikefish* on August 13, 1945. And Commander B. E. Lewellen of the *Torsk* sank two coastal-defense vessels on August 14, only a few hours before the war ended.

It was a costly campaign for the submariners. Out of a force whose average strength was 14,750 officers and men, 374 officers and 3131 men lost their lives. Fifty-two of our 288 submarines were lost, forty-one of them sunk by enemy action. But the other side of the picture was a proud one.

Between the first sinking by the *Swordfish* and the last by the *Torsk*, our submarines downed more than half of all the Japanese merchant and naval shipping sent to the bottom during World War II. More than a quarter of the enemy warships sunk by all agencies in the Pacific fell to our torpedoes, among them a battleship, four carriers, four escort carriers, three heavy cruisers, nine light cruisers, twenty-three submarines, and forty-three destroyers. In addition, our undersea fighters carried out countless special missions, including troop transport, lifeguard actions, reconnaissance, shore bombardments, mine laying, rescue missions, and support of guerrilla operations.

This record was scored by a service comprising less than two per cent of the personnel of the United States Navy.

We had come a long way from the L-boats of a generation before, that little handful of American undersea craft that served a purely defensive function in the fight against the German U-boats of World War I. Those boats were small and unstable; they lurched badly in rough seas; they were able to remain on patrol for an average of only about eight days at a time. The air in them was bad, the temperature that of the water outside, and moisture precipitated constantly on the insides of the vessels and dripped down on the crews like rain.

The fleet-type submarines of World War II — those, that is, that bore the names of fish — were palaces by comparison. We had air conditioning, movies, record players, ice-cream freezers, all the comforts of home within the narrow confines of our quarters. We could remain at sea for two and a half months or more and travel thousands of miles without refueling. Four diesel engines provided power for cruising on the surface and for charging the batteries that ran us when we were submerged. And we carried such death in our torpedo tubes as no World War I submariner ever dreamed of.

The effectiveness of our weapon was not the only factor of which we were ignorant as we cruised nervously off San Diego in the closing days of 1941. We were yet to learn the high compensations of our service.

The very nature of the Submarine Service produced an intimacy, an *esprit de corps,* and a spirit of romantic adven-

ture unmatched by the other branches and virtually forgotten in the massive maneuverings of modern war. In a
sense, we inherited the mantle of mystery, glamour, and
freedom of action worn by the airmen of World War I.
We were small, so small in the basic unit that every man
aboard a submarine knew every other man by his first name,
so small as a service that transfers, joint shore leaves, and
overlapping friendships tied us all together. We were spe-
cialists, engaged in far-ranging secret work for which no
real precedent existed in our naval history. And for all our
mutual interdependence, we were independent to a dramatic degree. That is where the romance came in.

The days of glory are long gone from most arenas of war.
Everything is in group and mass movements. Individuals,
even individual units, are increasingly lost from sight. But
the submarine kept its individuality. When we went out
on patrol, we were on our own. There was no one outside
the unit to give orders on how to make the approach, how
to attack, how to follow through. It was us against the
enemy. Sometimes we went out in wolfpacks, but in most
cases we were by ourselves. We had an area to patrol, and
we were given general instructions as to what to do or
what to expect, and within these orders we operated in an
area of great latitude. We were corsairs, in a world that
had almost forgotten the word. For all the grimness of war,
it was a thrilling and unique experience.

In our small ships' companies, every one of the eighty to
ninety men aboard had to depend on every other, and the
lowliest seaman had to be just as capable at his job as the
captain. In all warfare men depend on their comrades at

arms for their own safety, but in submarines this depend-
ence was magnified. Although rank was observed, there was
little formality and a great feeling that we were all on the
same team. We were singularly free of petty jealousies
among the crew, resentment by the men against the officers, or antagonism by the officers toward the men. On the
Pollack, when I was aboard her, a talented radioman drew
good-natured cartoons lampooning the officers in the ship's
newspaper. On the *Wahoo*, it was an enlisted man who provided Mush Morton the key to Wewak harbor.

I remember a night when I was standing on the bridge of
my own submarine, the *Flasher*, plowing through a calm
sea with the moon shining, scanning the horizon in company with a lookout for a sight of the enemy, when I was
struck with an almost mystical conviction that every man
below was my brother. The words from *Henry V* came
back to me: "For he today that sheds his blood with me
shall be my brother." It was a feeling that I think all of us
shared. To this day, when I see a man wearing a submarine
pin, I stop him and wring his hand.

I don't know who pinned the title "The Silent Service"
on us, but for all its aptness it inevitably proved somewhat
misleading. Submarine operations were cloaked in secrecy,
with a few exceptions for the benefit of morale, like the
public acclaim given Mush Morton when we got back from
the patrol in which the *Wahoo* made its famous "reconnaissance" of Wewak harbor. And the title conveyed some
of the mystery and glamour of the service to a public that
knew virtually nothing of submarines. On the other hand,

it helped develop a picture of submariners as grim, tight-lipped men of a different breed from the others, and this of course was a mistake.

To me, the Submarine Service was not grim in any sense of the word. Some of the experiences were grim, for many of the subs went through hell, but the image called up by the adjective is misleading when it is applied to the men. Submariners were close-mouthed by necessity rather than by nature. But at any given moment aboard a submarine in action, the atmosphere was as likely to be burlesque as tragic. Submariners had a beautifully developed sense of humor; they needed it.

In fact, I think too little has been said generally about the American sense of humor during wartime. It was a sort of secret weapon for us all. I remember reading a captured report of a Japanese patrol submarine which had been off Pearl Harbor on December 7, 1941. Its officers thought they had been caught in a submarine net. They hit bottom, somewhere off Hawaii, and the boat took such a terrible down-angle at one point that their latrines overflowed and flooded every compartment. The report said the Japanese sailors grimly stood and toasted the Emperor before they made what they called their final death surface. They were convinced they were going to surface right in the face of the enemy and be annihilated. Actually, the report said, there was no enemy in sight when they surfaced, so they returned to the Empire.

Now, if an American crew had found themselves in that critical situation, and standing knee-deep in offal, the members would definitely not have toasted Franklin Delano

Roosevelt or talked about a death surface. They would have made a joke of it, as Captain Worth Scanland did when pretty much the same thing happened to us aboard the *Hawkbill* in 1944, and after surfacing they probably would have gone on into the harbor and shot somebody up.

When Bull Wright, after his first successful attack as skipper of the *Sturgeon*, sent his famous report, "STURGEON NO LONGER VIRGIN," it was more than a facile pun. When Red Cole, plagued by a shortage of toilet paper aboard the *Skipjack*, sent a deadpan communication through channels outlining the history of the emergency and detailing the field expedients employed, it was more than a hilarious blow at red tape. These things were evidences of a healthy mental condition that pervaded all our armed services, but was especially noticeable among the submariners.

For the grim truths of war were not the fuel that kept men going. They didn't relieve the tension; they built it up. The funny things *did* relieve tension. As a situation grew worse, you could almost see the whole boat tensing. And then something really funny would happen to bleed off the pressure, as it did on the *Pollack* one hazardous night when a lookout pinched our skipper's fanny by mistake, an incident of which more shall be recorded later.

It was the dental plate of an elderly submarine volunteer named Wach that made an especially rough moment on the *Wahoo* bearable. Roger Paine, my first friend among the officers of that great submarine, recalled it more than ten years later when we were reminiscing. Wach was an old man as submariners go, about forty, and on his first patrol. The *Wahoo* had had a good day off Honshu and was pulling away from the coast at deep depth and running silent, knowing the Japanese subchasers were on the prowl. Roger was in the forward torpedo room talking to Wach when an airplane dropped one of the enemy's new and highly touted blockbusters in the area. It was Wach's first experience of a depth charge, let alone a blockbuster, and he stopped talking in mid-sentence, mouth open and eyes wide — and his upper plate carried away and dropped down on the lower. Roger said the sight of this startled submariner standing there with his mouth open and his teeth shut was more than anyone in the torpedo room could stand. Depth charges or no, every man present doubled up and howled with glee.

I knew almost no one in subs whose sense of humor wasn't developed just a little better than it was in other people. We had to have it to survive. On the *Wahoo's* second patrol, we traveled for weeks with a torpedo jammed in its tube in such a way that we expected it to explode and blow us all up at any time. The ritual we developed, of going down to the tube every night, putting our ear to it, and bowing down to pay obeisance, was admittedly silly, and yet it made the situation endurable.

More than that, I believe humor served as an aid to discipline, the right kind of discipline. The purpose of discipline is to get the organization to work effectively as a unit; there is no other legitimate objective. And discipline unrelieved by humor will build up terrible tensions that defeat its purpose. The lookout who pinches an officer by accident and brings down a walloping wisecrack on his head instead of a stern rebuke will salute his captain with greater speed and respect the next time they are ashore — and, what is more to the point, will follow him more willingly in a crisis.

The stories passed from sub to sub also served to bind us even closer together. Part of the service's matchless morale, as I have indicated, came from our size. When the *Stingray* performed one of the most remarkable lifeguard exploits of the war, dragging an American airman out of range of enemy guns while he clung to the periscope of the submerged submarine, it meant more to me because the *Stingray's* skipper was Sam Loomis, an old friend. Dick O'Kane's fantastic exploits on the *Tang* were discussed with affectionate admiration by every man who had served with him on the *Wahoo*. When I became captain of the *Flasher*, the submarine that was to get credit for sinking more enemy tonnage than any other during the war, I already knew the fine record she had been making for herself under my good friend Reuben Whitaker — and I knew the story about Reuben's conversation with Bull Wright the night Pearl Harbor was attacked. Reuben was Bull's executive officer on the *Sturgeon* then, and when the electrifying message reached the *Sturgeon* in the Philippines, he rushed to Bull's stateroom with it. But the skipper had been out late at a party and had come in somewhat *hors de combat;* it was all Reuben could do to shake him half awake. Bull listened to the dispatch. "Okay, Reuben," he said, "you take care of it." Then he grunted sleepily and rolled over, satisfied at least for the moment that his exec could handle a little thing like a war.

On patrol we read the reports of the other subs, and

ashore we talked about them. Howard Gilmore, who gave his life for the *Growler* by ordering her down while he hung wounded on the bridge; Chester Smith of the *Swordfish*, who took President Quezon off the Philippines; Joe Enright of the *Archerfish*, who sank the largest man-of-war ever downed by a submarine; Gene Fluckey, who used his *Barb* for shore bombardments as well as for sinking enemy ships — we knew them all, or knew someone who did.

My own wartime experience covered patrols on the *Wahoo*, the *Pollack*, the *Hawkbill*, and the *Flasher*. Each had its own distinctive character as a boat and memorable shipmates, and never in any of the nine patrols I made on those four subs did we return empty-handed. It was my good fortune to know the magnificent Mush Morton at the very peak of his career, to watch Dick O'Kane develop the quality of command that won him the Medal of Honor, and to live and fight side by side with scores of other men equally valiant, some of whom had grown up in the peacetime Navy, others who had never even seen a submarine until they were grown men.

Whenever we got into a big naval base like Pearl Harbor, we would hear from men in other services the talk about the "ninety-day wonders" and the "trade-school boys" and get a hint of the jealousies and hostilities that sometimes existed between the reserves and the regulars. No such attitude ever existed on the subs I served on. I would be hard put now to recall which of my former comrades at arms were Naval Academy graduates and which were not. On the *Flasher*, I think, there were two Annapolis men besides myself out of nine officers. Certainly as a test of the

ability of an officer, the Academy ring was inconclusive.
There was a slightly greater accentuation of devotion to
routine duties among the so-called regular officers, but on
the other hand — and of course I am speaking in the broad-
est generalities — the reserves had greater initiative and were
better able to accept unorthodox ideas. In fact, many of the
innovations that came in during combat were originated by
men whose imagination was not bound by traditional con-
cepts of naval warfare.

There was something else that we in the Submarine Service held in common. We were participating in a kind of
warfare that, during World War I, our own families had
learned to abhor. "Unrestricted submarine warfare" was a
synonym for dishonor in the days when German U-boats
were at their peak, and even though total war was all about
us in the days after Pearl Harbor, from time to time someone would bring up the question of conscience.

Insofar as a distinction is made between the evils of submarine warfare and those of other forms of conflict, none
of us was disturbed by our role, though some may have been
unhappy at the attitude of friends on the point. Once you
embark on a policy of total warfare, the man who fires at
an unarmed merchant ship from below the surface is surely
no more culpable than the man who drops bombs on it from
above. And we were not in the role of monsters who struck
blows against helpless adversaries with impunity; there were
usually escorts lurking in the background, or boiling into
the center of the action. The casualty rate is enough to establish the fact that submariners underwent more hazards
than the average, rather than fewer.

During the war itself, my conscience never bothered me. We were aware that all the ships we torpedoed had men aboard them, but by some metamorphosis that takes place in time of combat, we thought of them not as individuals — that might well have been unbearable — but as "the enemy," a vague, unspecific, emotional concept which does not boil down to a pair of eyes looking at you.

For me, and I think for everyone else, it was easy to close the more personal area of my mind automatically. I used to feel an occasional twinge, more of sorrow than remorse, for fellow seamen who were being sunk. One night on the *Wahoo* when we were stalking a lone, damaged freighter after he had seen all the other ships in his convoy go down, one by one, I felt a sort of pity for the captain of that remaining ship, a man who had expended every ounce of boldness and daring that was possible in his futile attempt to escape us, but my feeling was not very deep. Indeed, if it had been, I would doubtless have finished out the war in a hospital, seeking help from a psychiatrist.

But there was one incident on the sixth war patrol of the *Flasher* that I shall never forget. We sighted a rather large sampan and attacked it by gunfire, setting it afire within sight of land, and after it appeared that all the crew had abandoned her, we went alongside to finish the job with a hand grenade. Tom McCants went up on the bow of the *Flasher* with the grenade, we put the bow almost against the small burning vessel, and he tossed the grenade aboard, hoping it would go down in the hold and knock a hole in her bottom.

When the explosion occurred, a man jumped up out of

the stern. He had been hidden behind the gunwales, a tattered figure with blood on him, and as he went over the side and splashed into the water, he looked at me where I was standing on the bridge. He looked me, George Grider, right in the eye with an expression of piercing accusation, and in that brief moment the war was an intolerably personal thing. I threw off the sensation soon enough, but it sank into some recess of my mind, and although it took a while to blossom, it is full grown now. Many a night I think of that poor man, who probably wasn't even a Japanese, who perhaps wasn't a combatant at all, whose sampan was doubtless his only livelihood. We had destroyed it, and in so doing had destroyed him and his friends. He had said it all to me, and had given me my deepest scar of the entire war, in that one flashing glance.

Even so, I feel no personal burden of guilt, and I think it would be wrong if I did. Certainly if it all had to be done again, I would do it. The guilt I feel is that of mankind as a whole, and similarly I think it would be wrong if I did not feel that.

In warfare we all sin, he who fires the weapon no more than he, or she, who pays the taxes or buys the war bonds or contributes the layer cakes to the USO. All the same, I am sorry that I had to be an instrument in that awesome destruction. Like many another veteran, when I am lying in the bed in the dark watches of the night I sometimes think of all the men who died, and of my part in it, and I wish it weren't that way.

But even on submarines, the greatest portion of the time by far was spent apart from actual combat. When the time

came, we might be at battle stations for twenty-four hours
or more at a stretch, and alerted for action for days or
weeks at a time. But those periods were infinitely short by
comparison with the total number of hours we spent on
patrol. And it was the rest of the time that helped us
remember we were human. I learned to love many factors of submarine life that had nothing to do with sinking
ships.

Of all my wartime jobs, the one that was the most pleasant and interesting was the job of navigator. I loved to navigate. There was something almost sensuously delightful
about the precision and exactitude with which you could locate your position out there in those empty wastes of ocean
by shooting stars and by using a beautifully made chro-
nometer to give you the exact fix. It is thrilling to go up in
daytime, figure out the position of Venus, look in that direction in the sky, and see a dim little pinpoint of light from
which you can fix your position. After days of running over
the open sea, a good navigator can say, "Tonight at six
o'clock we're going to sight such and such an island" — and,
by Heaven, when the time comes, there it is. There are few
endeavors in life that bring so concrete a reward.

And there was the strange peace, based ironically on the
feeling of accomplishment during patrol, that marked the
days when we were returning to port. We usually headed
for the barn with a conviction that while we might have
done better, we had not gone out and labored in vain. And
because of that, we could stand on the bridge and forget
the war for a while. When we got a couple of days' run
away from enemy waters, we were relatively safe; there

was always a chance we might be knocked off by an enemy sub, but it was remote, and as long as we remained alert the danger from planes was slight.

If you have ever seen a picture of a submarine coming up from beneath the surface, the water cascading off her bridge as she settles to an even keel, you may have guessed the strange feeling of closeness that develops between a submariner and the waters about him. For the submarine is very intimate with the ocean. It glides along like a beautiful arrow, quiet and powerful and more a part of the water than any other craft I know. To stand on its bridge as the sun is setting and watch its wake stretching astern to the horizon, knowing the brief pleasures of comfort, safety, and the satisfaction of a job done, is warming and, in a quiet way, exhilarating.

All this lay ahead of us in the confused days and nights our division of S-boats spent off San Diego. We were not yet even a real part of the drama already begun in the Pacific. But our adventure served a purpose. It kept us occupied without doing any harm, and when we returned to port, we were ready to steady down.

Ann was still in San Diego, a fact that incensed many officers of the division. All the other wives but one had packed up and left during our patrol, I suppose on the advice of their husbands, and at Coronado, across the bay from San Diego, practically every house was for sale. I was looked upon by my associates as revolting proof that improvidence sometimes pays.

We resumed our training program, the months passed,

the wives began to trickle back, and the price of real estate on Coronado soared. And at last, in March of 1942, I was ordered to the U.S.S. *Wahoo*, then building at Mare Island, California. Ann went home this time — her mother was critically ill — and I said good-by to S-boats forever and reported to the *Wahoo*.

2

Preparation

SHE WAS STILL on the ways. The only officer who had arrived ahead of me was Roger Paine, three years my junior at
the Naval Academy, a quiet, dark-haired, friendly man
who was to be the gunnery and torpedo officer. The two of
us went over to the *Whale*, a sub ahead of ours on the
schedule, and got acquainted with her officers. A couple of
them actually had been out and made a real war patrol before coming back to the *Whale*, and we listened to them
at every opportunity in the days that followed. They were
the gods of the submarine group at Mare Island: they had
encountered the enemy.

Our own officers began to report. Our captain was Lieutenant Commander Marvin Kennedy, a tall, thin man with
red hair, a pink complexion, and a fine reputation as an able
administrator who ran a taut ship. Our executive officer
was a young man who struck me as overly garrulous and
potentially unstable. His name was Dick O'Kane. He had
been fourth or fifth officer on the *Argonaut*, the biggest
submarine the Navy had yet built. Dick was likable and ob-

viously a hard worker, careful about details, but there was something about him that made us feel he was a little out of touch with reality. Still, we couldn't help listening when he told us about the *Argonaut*. It was a mine layer, and while it had not sunk any enemy ships, it had seen some, and that was quite a thing to us. Dick said he had recommended to the captain that they request permission to proceed to Japan and lay mines off the coast. His recommendation, he added impatiently, had been ignored. The story only confirmed our doubts about our new exec. I think now his mine-laying proposal was a good one, but at the time it sounded like the height of foolhardiness to all of us. I doubt if any of us would have believed then that Dick would come out of the war with a Congressional Medal of Honor and a wartime record almost unmatched in the Submarine Service.

I was the third officer on the *Wahoo*, after O'Kane. Roger Paine was the fourth, and Hank Henderson, a Virginian, was next in line. Later, Jack Griggs came aboard as my assistant, and George Misch reported as the most junior of the officers.

Our job, before the *Wahoo* was launched, was to supervise its construction. Building a boat (and I should explain that subs are usually, though not always, called boats rather than ships) is a lot different from building an automobile. Though the plans are carefully drawn, each sub turns out to be a distinct individual. Changes recommended as a result of combat experiences are constantly coming in, and modifications are adopted by the engineers or by the officers themselves. The Mare Island Navy Yard was a Navy installation, of course, and the boat was built by the Navy.

The builders were responsible, but they weren't the ones who were going out to fight in it. We were, and we wanted to make certain it was properly constructed. What's more, we wanted to know *how* it was constructed, every inch of it, so that when something went wrong, we would know what it was and where it was.

A submarine sailor, be he a seaman or the captain himself, probably knows more about his weapon, which is his boat, than any other fighting man. Certainly he knows it as well as an infantryman knows his rifle. Submariners are volunteers, every man and officer, and before they are accepted, they have to pass a test that is excruciating in its thoroughness. A man will be asked, for example, how to pump from the forward trim tank to the negative tank, how to blow water from the forward torpedo tubes to the after tubes, even how to flush the toilet with a trim pump. And if you think so small a thing as flushing the toilet is a simple matter, let me quote the flushing instructions on the *Wahoo:*

> Before using, see that Bowl Flapper Valve "A" is closed, Gate Valve "C" in discharge pipe line is open, Valve "D" in water supply line is open. Then open Valve "E" next to bowl to admit necessary water. Close Valves "D" and "E." After using Pull Lever "A," release Lever "A." Open Valve "C" in air supply line. Rock Air Valve Lever "F" outboard to charge measuring tank to ten pounds above sea pressure. Open Valve "B" and rock air valve lever inboard to blow overboard. Close Valves "B," "C," and "G."

All these details were important. There would come a time, on another submarine I served on, when difficulties with a valve in the forward torpedo-room head provided one of the most harrowing cases of valor in action that I witnessed during the war. The aromatic sacrifice of Ensign Rex Murphy will be recounted later.

I never worked harder in my life than I did during the building, commissioning, and testing of the *Wahoo*. We had a little shack of an office on the second floor of a wooden building in the Navy Yard — a building that had been thrown up for temporary use during World War I. It smelled of diesel oil and tired sailors, and, with its few desks and a typewriter and telephone, it was the nerve center from which the building of the boat was controlled.

As the crew came aboard, a few men at a time, we added to our building job the task of training the crew. Besides that, of course, we had to read the patrol reports, which were now coming in regularly, get our papers, codes, and charts in order, and test every piece of machinery. During this period the devoted service of a pharmacist's mate named Lindhe stood out like a beacon light. One of his accomplishments in particular should have earned him an official commendation, but actually it would have got him court-martialed if it had come to the attention of the wrong people.

Lindhe, an extraordinarily resourceful man, had become our unofficial procurer-of-scarce-parts. If we needed anything we couldn't get through Navy channels, all we had to do was turn him loose and ask no questions when he returned. On this particular occasion we were desperately in need of a piece of equipment for our radar. It is hard now to realize how supersecret that sort of thing was back in 1942 — secret and agonizingly slow to obtain through channels. One of our tubes, about half the size of a football, had blown out, and we had to have a replacement in a hurry, for we were about ready to leave Mare Island. It would have taken weeks to get a new tube by orderly processes, so we called Lindhe in, let him know of our needs, and offered him a day's leave.

He was back that night with the tube.

Later, we learned in outline how he did it, though I suppose the details will never be known. He had gone over to the Naval Supply Depot at Oakland, a heavily guarded place where no ordinary sailor was ever allowed, and got in. He had gone to the right warehouse and got the tube we needed. Then his only problem was how to get away from the depot with it.

A foreign agent might have laid plans for months for the accomplishment of this hazardous feat, and still failed. Lindhe simply made friends with the driver of a truck loaded with soft drinks, hid his precious tube among dozens of bottles of Coca-Cola, and brought it out the main gate.

I still think Lindhe should have gone into Intelligence. Not that he wasn't a fine sailor; he was. But as pharmacist's mate he was also our ship's doctor, and it was a job to which he was not suited by temperament. It was to cause him terrible anguish during the *Wahoo*'s third war patrol. A 20-millimeter shell exploded on deck one day and mangled a sailor's toe badly. Lindhe was called to amputate the toe. He withdrew with his patient, there was a long wait, and then Lindhe returned, blinking back his tears. "I can't do it!" he choked. "I can't *do* it!" He finally did, of course, using some instrument that looked like a pair of pliers, but it hurt the surgeon more than the patient. Lindhe was a fine fighting man, but he simply could not stand the sight of blood.

At last the *Wahoo* was ready to go to sea.

The strain had been hard on everyone. We were worn out from overwork, nobody had had enough sleep for weeks, and we had been living constantly with the thought of the great unknown ahead of us. The last night before we left the Navy Yard, after the acceptance trials had been passed, we tied up to the dock in San Francisco, and the strain proved a little too much for our quartermaster.

Perhaps I should say the relaxation from strain was to blame. As our departure time approached, the sailors had made enthusiastic use of their rare opportunities to relax by going ashore and tanking up. This night the quartermaster, a tremendous, muscular man named Morgan, made the mistake of relaxing while he had the deck watch.

I was sleeping the sleep of exhaustion when I heard a messenger come down and try to wake Dick O'Kane. Dick and I shared the same stateroom, a space about the size of a Pullman roomette, with three bunks in it. Dick wouldn't wake up and I couldn't get back to sleep until the messenger quieted down, so I sat up and asked him what the trouble was.

"Morgan's up on deck, sir," he reported nervously, "and he's shooting out the lights on the dock with his .45."

Dick went right on snoring.

Weary, angry, and a little apprehensive, I dragged myself out and went up on deck. Sure enough, there was Morgan, waving his .45 around like a small boy with a water pistol. I approached him tentatively.

"Morgan," I said, "give me that gun."

He waved it in my direction and gave me a leer right out of the movies.

I tried to maneuver him over to the side, hoping that if he really aimed it at me, I could push him overboard and jump in after him. I had been on the swimming team at Annapolis, and at that moment I felt more confident in the water than out.

But the crisis passed. Morgan subsided. After a minute or so he turned over his gun and I ordered him below, hoping that would end it.

It didn't. He headed straight for the crew's mess, which is a sort of clubroom on a submarine, with two or three men always sitting around drinking coffee at any hour. He found someone who would listen and began holding forth on the *Wahoo* (a lousy boat), the Navy (a lousy branch), and everybody in general (he was going to get even with them). I went back and ordered him to turn in again.

A few minutes later he had returned, cursing and yelling. I called the messenger who had waked me in the first place.

"Get out the handcuffs," I said bitterly.

Submarines carry handcuffs and leg chains, though I had never seen them used before and never saw them used later. But I was tired, and sick to death of the sound of Morgan's voice. I took him up on deck and handcuffed him to the radio mast, which rose out of the afterdeck. Then I broke out the firehose and put it on the pump, and put the messenger on the hose.

"If he so much as opens his mouth," I said, "turn the hose on him." Then I went below, intending to sleep about an hour and come back up and send Morgan to bed.

The next I knew, it was seven o'clock in the morning.

I leaped out of the bunk and dashed up on deck. Morgan was slumped down before the radio mast, half asleep, his hands swollen to twice their normal size. Navy regulations swam before my eyes, especially those calling for the captain's orders and various other safeguards before any man is ever chained. Torn between horror at my own act and conviction that my naval career was ending before it was well begun, I got Morgan out of the handcuffs in a matter of seconds.

"Well," I said, trying to make my voice crisp with authority, "I think you've learned your lesson, haven't you?"

"Yessir." The poor fellow had a whale of a hangover.

"All right, Morgan," I went on kindly. "I'll never mention this to the captain."

My hope, of course, was that he'd never mention it either, and as our eyes met we reached a mutual understanding and agreement. It saved both of us a lot of trouble. Months later during our second war patrol, when he virtually saved the boat through a feat of almost superhuman strength, I appreciated his tremendous muscles far more than I had that night on deck.

From San Francisco, the *Wahoo* proceeded to San Diego, where we held intensive wartime training. We fired torpedoes, made practice approaches on target ships, and on a schedule that would have broken the heart of Hercules, we trained the crew of the *Wahoo*. Kennedy was a perfectionist and a slave driver. He demanded the utmost of every man on board, and he got it, because we knew how important it was to learn. Already we were telling one another that when we got to sea we were going to be the most successful damned submarine in the whole war. But it was a killing period, for our families as well as ourselves.

Ann had returned. She and Billy had been with me at Mare Island the last few weeks we were there, and now they joined me at San Diego. They stayed at Coronado again, along with a lot of the other submarine wives, and all of them suffered through the anxiety and strain of seeing the husbands who were about to leave them grow daily more exhausted and bad-tempered. It must have been hard on all the wives, just keeping the peace when we were ashore. One night, I remember, Ann and I went to a night club and I had a fight with a headwaiter simply because I thought he had kicked a dog. We were on the fine edge of exhaustion all around, training all day and working all night as often as not on the defects that had turned up during the day, knowing that if we didn't have everything in perfect shape when we left, it might be too late.

It was exhaustion of this sort, I suppose, that led to the flooding of the *Wahoo*'s magazine, a mishap that may well be unique in submarine annals. We were tied up to the dock in San Diego with all our ammunition aboard when it happened, just a day or so before we were supposed to leave.

The magazine has a flooding system which you can open

in event of fire to save it from exploding. Someone had inadvertently turned the wrong valve.

The first hint we had of it was in the morning, when we noticed that the boat was sitting about six inches deeper in the water than it should have been. It didn't take long to find the reason. Then we were confronted with the touchy problem of who was going to tell Pinky. Through some sort of lottery which I still believe was rigged, the job fell to me.

The captain was just as tired as everybody else, and he had long since established his complete intolerance toward carelessness. We didn't know what he would say, but we were all prepared for roars that would rattle the bulkheads. I looked at my fellow officers in bitter reproach and then went forward and saluted.

"Good morning, Captain," I said, wondering how I could work up gradually to the shattering news.

"Morning, Grider." He was edgy and impatient.

"Captain," I blurted, hurling subtlety to the winds, "I want to report the magazine is flooded."

For a lesser catastrophe, Pinky might have roasted us all. But a flooded magazine is such a cataclysmic event, such an utterly unbelievable thing to happen, that the magnitude of it did the trick. It stunned him.

"Very well," he said, in the empty tone of one talking in his sleep. "Let's pump it out." He might have been approving a change on the menu.

We got our pumps and a fire engine on it, and pumped it out. Then we had to take out every round of ammunition, every 50-caliber, every 20-millimeter, every 4-inch shell, and dry them off, and oil them, and dry out the cans the big ammunition was in, and then put everything back where it was. It took about a day and a half, and we did it without missing a minute of our schedule. When we left San Diego a couple of days later, we were dry, well armed, well trained, and practically walking in our sleep.

No one discussed it at the time, but the thing uppermost in all our minds, as it developed in later conversations, was fear. Not so much fear of the enemy as fear that we would turn out to be cowards. I don't know how a man can tell whether he is brave or not until he has been under fire, and hardly any of us had been.

Over and over during that last training period, I kept asking myself not whether I would be killed or wounded, but whether I would be afraid. I was deathly afraid already that when the depth charges went off or when some other emergency arose, I would panic and be unable to perform my duties. And the duties of any man on a submarine are complex. In my own case, as the diving officer, I was responsible for the trim of the boat, for diving, for maintaining neutral buoyancy through changing the amounts of water in the ballast tanks. These are tasks that require mental alertness and a considerable degree of coolness. Once, under the strain of weariness at San Diego, I had come to a morning when I was simply unable to figure out the morning trim. I was too exhausted to make even the most basic calculations required. What, I wondered, would happen when to exhaustion were added all the confusions and emotions of attack?

It is this kind of apprehension, I believe, that lies behind a great deal of the hilarity and almost insane shouting and laughing that takes place after a successful engagement with the enemy. Primarily, it is a form of self-congratulation: each man is relieved and triumphant because he has turned out not to be a coward.

Like the other officers aboard, too, I felt the burden of living up to the traditions of the Naval Academy and the Navy itself. We were officers; we had good reputations thus far; we were proud of them and scared to death we wouldn't live up to them.

During our training period, when we occasionally came across men who had been on war patrols and heard their casual references to being depth-charged or to firing torpedoes at the enemy, it filled us with awe. We didn't let them know we were impressed, but we were. And, in a way, we were maddened by the offhand way they talked. My Lord, I remember thinking, if I am ever on a boat that sinks an enemy ship, and if I do my duty, I'll be satisfied for life. And they're so casual about it!

Added to all this self-searching was our natural worry for our wives and families, left behind for the terrible waiting, and our concern over their future. In those early months there was an overwhelming feeling that nobody was going to come back. Now and then it found dramatic expression. I remember one man who, when he left, handed his wife an envelope marked with stern pessimism: *"Not to Be Opened until My Death."*

The poor girl opened it the day he left, naturally enough, and found in it solemn directives as to how she should live her life, how she should raise their fatherless children, and how she should remember him during her years of widowhood. I doubt that it helped her morale very much. Her husband, incidentally, came out of the war unscathed.

Later on, the feeling that this was going to be an Armageddon disappeared. After I made my first patrol or two, I seldom again thought consciously that I would be lost. Neither did the other men, and I don't think the wives did either. We had shifted from unreasonable pessimism to equally unreasonable optimism. But that was to come later; when we left San Diego and headed for action, we were a grim and keyed-up crew. We had said our last farewells. We had reached our moment in history. We were launched into the unknown.

Another and bigger unknown remained locked within us. The key lay somewhere in the South Pacific.

3

Attack

ALL I EVER SAW of the first ship we sank was a wisp of smoke and a dark shape on the horizon. That was nearly a month after our first patrol began, and two weeks after we had lost our first target.

The *Wahoo* had arrived at Pearl early in August and remained there for two weeks of intensive advanced training. Then, toward the end of the month, we left with orders to proceed to Truk, a group of islands in the Carolines, then regarded as perhaps the most dangerous bastion the Japanese had in the Pacific and the key to their easternmost naval defenses.

It is worth noting here that ideas about what a submarine should do on a war patrol had changed drastically since the bombing of Pearl Harbor. Most of our prewar training had been conducted with the idea that a sub would be a scouting vessel proceeding ahead of the fleet — a pattern of thinking influenced by the Battle of Jutland in World War I and by other engagements between major units of fleets. It was thought that a submarine's major function was to pro-

ceed a day or so ahead of the fleet, make the initial contact
with the enemy, maintain that contact, send back reports,
and conduct attacks in conjunction with our own forces.
After the bulk of our Pacific Fleet was either sunk or dis-
abled at Pearl, however, it became evident that this sort of
strategy would not be feasible. We *had* no fleet. By the
time the *Wahoo* went on her first patrol, the strategy was
to attack and sink any enemy shipping, be it warship or
merchantman. As a matter of fact, events were to prove this
was by far the most valuable function the submarines could
perform. By the end of the war, our undersea boats had
sunk more tonnage than Japan controlled when hostilities
began.

Our mission, then, was to proceed to our assigned area at
Truk, to patrol it, and to sink any and all Japanese naval or
merchant ships we encountered. We knew Truk was a hot
spot and we felt honored to be sent there; we were trained
to a hair-trigger edge and tremendously keyed up as we
absorbed our two final indoctrinal depth charges from our
escort and departed Pearl for our first taste of action. This
was it. The enemy lay ahead.

But action was not to come as soon as we thought. For
six days, as we approached our destination, nothing happened. On the seventh, our radar made an airplane contact
and we submerged so promptly that none of us even had
time to become nervous. Twice more in the next three days
we went under to avoid aircraft; then, on the twelfth day,
we reached our assigned area and began our periscope patrol.

The long days virtually without action had begun to

show on us. We had grown irritable, uncertain of ourselves, uneasy of our function and of our ability to fulfill it. But these moods vanished on the fourteenth day. After two full weeks of anticipation, we sighted our first target.

It was a small freighter of the *Hyogo Maru* class, about fifteen miles off Truk, headed for Piaanu Pass, which was known generally to our forces as Piano Pass. The time was shortly before daylight, and we were patrolling on the surface, recharging our batteries. At last my opportunity had come to test myself as diving officer under combat conditions.

Imagine two small rooms, one on top of the other, and a sun porch on top of both, and you have the nerve center of a submarine during a war patrol. The sun porch is the bridge, manned by the officer of the deck and his lookouts when the submarine is on the surface. Directly below it is the conning tower, a tiny auxiliary hull built above the boat's principal hull, about twelve feet long and eight across, holding all the controls by which the boat can be "conned" and operated submerged. And directly below the conning tower is the slightly larger control room, which houses all the diving controls.

At battle stations, virtually every officer aboard except the diving officer is crowded into the conning tower. The diving officer stands in the control room at the foot of the ladder from the conning tower and carries out the orders shouted down the hatch by the captain.

The signal for this first combat dive of the *Wahoo* came from the bridge: two raucous blasts of a klaxon, strident *Ooga! Ooga!* sounds carried into every compartment of the boat. It is a noise that makes your spine tingle every time you hear it, and this time my mouth went dry at the sound. I looked around the crowded little room, wondering if the men under my command guessed how nervous I was. In that first moment it didn't occur to me that they must be equally nervous.

The chief of the boat — the chief petty officer — moved first. His station was at the hydraulic manifold, which controls the opening and shutting of the vents. As the alarm sounded, he reached out automatically to open vents on all tanks. In front of him, at face level, was the Christmas Tree, a board with red and green lights for every vital opening in the hull and all the ballast-tank vents.

It all took only seconds, by contrast with the two or three minutes required in my prewar days on the *Skipjack*, for the entire routine had been streamlined. As the chief was opening the vents, the two lookouts came tumbling down the ladder to take their posts as planesmen, controlling the big fins at bow and stern which, like the elevators on an airplane, tilt to control the boat's depth and angle in a dive. As the bow planesman began to rig out the bowplanes, I turned my attention back to the Christmas Tree.

You need air to run the diesel engines that drive the boat on the surface. Submerged, without an unlimited air supply, you must operate on batteries. At the sound of the diving alarm, the engines had been stopped in the engine room; now the chief waited for an indicator to show that they were off, so he could close the main induction valve.

Green light on the Christmas Tree for the main induction valve. . . .

I waited then for the conning tower hatch light to go from red to green. A heavy thump told me the hatch was closed, and I knew Morgan, the quartermaster, was dogging it down with the hand wheel. Fifteen seconds from the sound of the alarm and it was done.

"Green board," the chief reported.

All the vital openings had now been shut. The main ballast-tank vents would remain open until we were under. The chief opened the bow buoyancy tank and the negative tank, the boat became suddenly heavy, and down we went.

At my back stood a man at the high-pressure air manifold, a bank of valves controlling the compressed air blown to the tanks. I signaled to him now, and he let high-pressure air escape into the boat while I watched for the pressure to build up on the barometer. It did, and it stayed up, so I knew the hull was airtight.

"Pressure in the boat, sir."

"Very well. Level off at sixty-five feet." We were going under just to periscope depth.

The needle crept around the dial on the depth gauge. Twenty feet . . . thirty . . . forty-five . . .

"Blow negative . . . shut negative flood . . . vent negative inboard . . . shut main ballast-tank vents . . ."

Above us, in the conning tower, the helmsman had signaled on the Motor Order Telegraph for one-third speed so we could get the feel of the boat. You need to know whether it is heavy or light, down by the bow or down by the stern, whether you're going to have to pump water from one end of the boat to the other to trim it fore and aft, whether you're going to have to flood water into the trim tanks to make the boat heavier, or pump it out to make it lighter.

I should emphasize that the operation did not look nearly as dramatic as it may sound. Everyone was nonchalant, casual almost to a studied degree. The orders and responses came in undertones. Some were never even spoken: from long association, we communicated by hand signals or facial expressions. But there was plenty of ferment inside us, for diving a boat calls for extreme precision. It is not at all unusual during an attack for the captain to yell down to the diving officer, "Take it down another six inches!"

We were down, and down well. Now we awaited orders from the conning tower, where the approach was being worked out like a mathematical problem, and I had time to worry about what would happen when we fired our torpedoes.

When you fire the bow tubes, there is a strong tendency for the boat to broach; that is, for its bow to come up out of the water. If your target has an escort, that can be fatal. So I worried about that, and generally about the way I was running my part of the job, and, in a secondary way, about what the Japanese might do to us. Men going into their first attack always endow the enemy with superhuman knowledge and skill. It takes a long time before you adopt the attitude that the odds are on your side. In retrospect, of course, that was just a poor lonesome freighter, and he was probably scared to death, but in 1942, on our first attack, we didn't feel that way about him at all.

We fired three torpedoes at the freighter, at a range of 1430 yards. Then, after a couple of minutes, we turned toward the target, went deep, ran under it, and kept going. He had turned toward us just after we fired, and we were reasonably sure he was unhit, though we heard the sound of an explosion — perhaps a defective torpedo or a depth charge dropped in fright by the target. But an aerial escort had been sighted through the periscope just before we fired, so rather than risk trouble we left it at that.

And that was the end of it. After the exhausting months of drills, after the build-up of tension within each man as to how he would conduct himself in danger, it was demoralizing to creep away submerged from that first target. The faint hope that maybe we had scored a hit after all, though we would never know it, only made the bitterness and disappointment worse.

We sighted another ship eight days later, a small freighter, but he was six miles away and we were unable to get in on him. On September 20, after we had been on station seventeen days and seen only two small ships, we decided to change our position. We had been patrolling well out on the approaches to Piano Pass; now we decided to head south.

And, as it happened, I was officer of the deck that same night when Bird-Dog Keeter sighted smoke.

We were running on the surface, recharging our batteries, and there were three lookouts on the bridge with me, each with a third of the horizon's circle to watch. Keeter, behind me on the cigarette deck, had the after third.

Motor Machinist's Mate D. C. Keeter was a good man to have on lookout, for he was one of the most alert lookouts

I ever saw. He had a habit of freezing every now and then, like a good pointer that has come on a covey of quail, while he studied some speck on the horizon. At first it was distracting; you would forget to watch anything but Keeter, waiting to see him go on point. But it was a fine example of concentration on the job, and it paid off that night. Keeter froze, pointed, and sang out:

"Smoke on the horizon. Bearing one hundred and twenty starboard."

We turned toward it in the bright moonlight. I watched long enough to make out a dim hull shape before I called the captain and ambled with studied unconcern down to the control room. It was the first enemy ship I had actually seen.

It was a freighter of the *Keiyo Maru* class, 6500 tons, as it turned out, and we ran toward it for half an hour on the surface and then submerged for a periscope attack. He seemed to be on a southeastward course, making about twelve knots, but every now and then he would stop and lie to. After a while we guessed why: he was waiting for his escort. At five minutes after midnight, when our tracks were very close together, we began to swing left for a stern tube shot.

All this time, of course, I was down in the control room. The only hint we had of what was going on was what we could pick up by listening to the captain's words as they drifted down the hatch, and to the words of the telephone talker near him in the conning tower. But it was obvious that the picture was a cloudy one to the entire fire-control party. Even by moonlight, making a periscope approach at night is a difficult and haphazard sort of affair. All that can be seen through the periscope is a blob, and it is easy to lose it or to misjudge its angle.

Suddenly, as we swung around, we began to hear pings on the sound operator's loudspeaker.

Someone was echo-ranging, and freighters don't have echo-ranging equipment. Up there in the moonlight, then, an escort ship was sending out sonar signals. If they bounced off our hull loud enough for him to pick up the echo, he would have us spotted.

I don't want to use the word claustrophobia, because I've never felt that or known anyone who did on a submarine, but as those ominous pings began we did have a sensation of groping — a lonely feeling that we were blind, unsafe because we couldn't see, and that somewhere up there a destroyer, a ship built to sink subs, was looking for us.

"Stand by to fire."

The words were low in the conning tower, but in the silence of the control room every man could hear them, and every man breathed a sigh of relief. The captain had what he decided was a good setup, the outer doors were opened on the torpedo tubes, the long wait was almost over.

"Stand by for final bearing. . . ." And again that sudden dryness in the mouth.

"Mark bearing . . . set . . . fire One!"

The boat shuddered as the first torpedo went out. Then, at the captain's commands, it was followed by a second, and a third.

We were firing from the freighter's starboard quarter, three quarters of the way around from the bow. But he swung left just as we fired – probably by chance, for it is more than likely that at that moment neither he nor his escort even knew we were there. The fact we could hear the escort's pinging did not necessarily mean he had contacted us; indeed, the continuing cycle of louder and then softer pings indicated he was merely scanning the area and had not yet spotted us. Still, he might pick us up at any second, and we didn't even know where he was.

The torpedoes missed, all three of them.

But the turn that had saved the target from them was also to be his doom. Round and round he swung until we were off his port beam.

"Fire Four!"

Again the boat shuddered, and again we waited. That torpedo's run should have been a minute and twenty seconds. A short time, but as you listen, it is an eternity.

The periscope was down now. All action had halted. Silent, suspended in the water, we waited . . .

Boom!

First came the loud explosion. The breaking-up noises followed, small explosions piling one on top of another, sounds that made you see bulkheads caving in, water pouring through great jagged wounds in the hull. We heard the first explosion through the hull of the submarine itself; the smaller ones came over the listening equipment in the conning tower, but they were loud enough.

That one hit was sufficient. We picked up the freighter in the periscope again in time to see him listing heavily to port. Before we left the scene, he had sunk.

*   *   *

Now came the punishment. The periscope, swinging around, picked up the escort, a small destroyer, with a bone in his teeth, headed right at us.

"Down periscope! Flood negative!"

We started for deep submergence, trying to get deep and away from that spot. For the moment, we weren't trying to be quiet, as we had during the tedious moments of the approach and the attack. All we wanted now was to get somewhere else, and fast.

"Rig for depth-charge attack."

Now was the time to get quiet again. Every piece of machinery that made any noise, everything we could do without, was cut off. The air conditioning, installed to protect electrical equipment, stopped circulating its cooling breeze. The heat of engines, motors, and relays began to creep through the boat. The planesmen and helmsmen, who had been controlling electric motors, shifted to hand control; the sweat poured down them now as they strained to turn and control the giant fins and rudder by the strength of their own backs. The flappers in the bulkheads and on the ventilation system were closed, so that if a compartment was flooded, it could be isolated — an empty gesture, as we all knew, because any flooded compartment will sink you in deep water.

And then, while we were still going down and going fast, even before we were mentally prepared for it, the first depth charge went off.

It was the worst, because the escort still knew just about where we were. We could hear — through the hull this time, not on the listening gear — the propellers of the freighter's avenger going overhead. And suddenly, on the sound gear, we heard a splash. The first depth charge had hit the water.

An exploding depth charge has three noises. First there is a click. Then comes a clang or crashing sound, like someone hitting your hull with a million sledgehammers. Finally there is a swishing noise, as though water is falling over a waterfall or pouring into a cavity the charge has created. The closer the charge is, the more closely together these noises come. When it is very close, you hear one horrible *clang*.

The first one was that way. Cork and paint chipped off the bulkheads. A light bulb shattered near my head. The boat shook. There was the jarring, head-swimming, detached feeling such as you get in an automobile crash, or from a stiff right to the jaw, a feeling that this is happening to you, all right, but that you are somehow above and away from it in spirit, looking down objectively at your body, which is taking the punishment.

He dropped about a dozen charges before we began creeping away from him, running deep and silent and a little dazed. If we could get a couple of miles away, we thought, we could lose him in the darkness, surface in safety, and sneak away.

We eased farther and farther from the depth charges and surfaced about a mile from him. He sighted us in a minute, and started at us.

There was a rain squall on the horizon, and we headed for it at full speed. Rain squalls were very helpful in such a situation, especially at night. Once we were on the surface and running away from him, his sound equipment was practically useless for finding us, and we could make much better speed than we could submerged as we ran for cover. Of course, when we went fast the boat threw up a luminous wake — in some areas of the Pacific you can stand in the after part of the bridge and read a newspaper at midnight from the wake of your boat — but the rain squall would hide us and our wake long enough to lose him.

At least that was the plan, and it worked. He was closing on us as we entered the squall, but he was not close enough to do anything, and we changed course and came out the other side. In a little while he was out, too, but by then we had skirted around and were ready to enter it from another place. This time, when we came out, we had lost him. Our eerie game of hide-and-seek there on the darkened ocean had ended; our prize for winning was our lives.

Looking back on it later, that first attack and depth-charging were to seem almost laughably tame. But at the time we were drunk with exhilaration and pride.

We had finally sunk a ship, after all the weeks of heartbreak and effort and waiting and watching, after all the fighting of boredom and fear. It wasn't a big ship, but it was ours. And we had been depth-charged, and we had come through, not merely with our lives but with our honor. Everyone was pounding everyone else on the back, everyone was a little wild-eyed, and below the surface you could feel the swelling tides of relief: the exultant realization that each of us had done his duty, that none of us had broken down, that we had at last explored the mysteries of our own souls and found there what we had hoped to find.

4

Anticlimax

UNTIL NOW, as I suppose it is with all men approaching their
first combat test, we had been preoccupied with ourselves,
our boat, and our own few miles of ocean. We were aware
of larger events going on about us in the vastness of the Pacific; our briefings at Pearl Harbor had assured that, and
the daily newscasts and code messages we got by radio on
the *Wahoo* kept us generally informed. But "the big picture" remained only a phrase until, by the actual firing of
torpedoes, the sinking of enemy tonnage, and the survival of
enemy attack, we had ourselves become a part of it.

Now the empty miles of ocean, which before had only
heightened our isolation and introspection, joined us to the
other fighting. We were oriented at last. The spot where
our freighter went down was like one of two marks between which a straight line is drawn. The other mark, toward which we now looked with new understanding, was
named Guadalcanal.

It was late September, 1942. Guadalcanal had become the
bloody symbol of all our hopes that the Japanese surge of

conquest might be halted and even thrown back. During the previous spring, we had been buoyed up by the costly naval victories of Coral Sea and Midway, both of great strategic importance, but Guadalcanal was something different. For the first time since the war began, a definite counteroffensive was under way. The Marines had landed August 7, and the fighting by land, sea, and air still continued with relentless intensity.

So it was because of Guadalcanal that we were roaming the sea lanes near Truk, so many miles away from the conflict. For, from their bastion at Truk, the Japanese were pouring supplies and warcraft into the holocaust in the Solomons, and every ton of shipping we sank here was a blow toward the conquest of Guadalcanal. Now that we could see ourselves as part of that conflict, we were on fire to find and sink new targets.

Instead, we almost sank ourselves with one of our own torpedoes.

Even on combat patrols, we were required to conduct routine tests on the torpedo tubes every night to assure that they were always in a state of readiness. On the second night after our attack, something went wrong.

A torpedo is ejected from its tube by air pressure. There is a massive door at each end of the tube; to fire the torpedo, you flood the tube, open the outboard door, charge the impulse tank to great air pressure, and then blast torpedo, water, and air out the tube. In the nightly checks of the fish a different procedure, known as firing inboard slugs, is followed. Since you are merely testing the equipment, you leave the outboard door shut, open the inner door, trip an elaborate system of protective interlocking devices, and fire the tube. The torpedo remains in place and a blast of air comes back into the boat through the dry tube.

That is what should have happened when **Roger Paine** turned out his torpedo crew on the night in question, but it didn't. A torpedoman second class named Myers inadvertently altered the procedure. He had the inner door of tube four open and ready for the slug test and had charged the correct impulse tank, when he made his mistake. He lifted the safety interlock on tube six, rather than four, and pushed the firing lever. Tube six was one of our surface ready tubes, set for instant action. Its impulse tank was charged, too, and *both* its doors were closed.

This happened as poor Roger was moving from the after to the forward torpedo room. Just as he stepped into the forward room, there was a sharp jolt, as if the boat had bumped a log, and Myers rushed to meet him.

"I think I just fired the fish in tube six," he said.

Roger, as he told us later, was somewhat shook. He ran forward and cracked the inboard vent on tube six, getting a little air and then water. The sight glass on the inner door showed the tube was full of water. It was evident the fish was still in the tube, but just how far in he couldn't tell from inside.

While this situation was developing in the forward torpedo room, Hank Henderson and I were standing watch as officers of the deck without a care in the world. The *Wahoo* was lying to, virtually motionless in the moonlit water, the muffled throb of her diesels on battery charge only emphasizing the peaceful quiet about us. I felt the strange thump underfoot and was puzzled enough to wander back aft and ask Hank, whose post was only about ten feet from mine, if he had noticed it. We talked about it for a minute or two with complete unconcern and I returned forward.

And there in the water just at the bow were two strange shapes. They couldn't be bits of driftwood; if so, we would have seen them long ago. Moreover, they were moving, bobbing about like some strange marine life. I gripped the rail and tried to recall whether seals had ever been reported in the western Pacific.

The captain popped out of the hatch and stood stiffly, looking forward. He seemed to be under great tension, but he showed no surprise at the weird shapes. It was too much for me. "Captain," I ventured, "those two shapes in the water. Think they're seals, sir?"

"No," he snapped, "they're not seals. They're Paine and Smith."

In the few moments I had been aft, Roger had reported to the captain, gained permission to go over the side to see what had happened, and grabbed the coxswain, Donald Smith, to help. They had dashed topside, run forward to the bow, and plunged into the water while I was talking to Hank.

Roger's frantic speed was inspired by his knowledge of the ticklish nature of torpedoes in general, and his almost certain conviction that this one was stuck part way out the tube. Sometimes a torpedo will damage its rudder when it is fired. If this happens, it may circle back and hit its mother ship. To minimize the possibility of this disaster, each fish has on the underside of its warhead a little paddle wheel that is turned by the water as the torpedo moves. Until the paddle wheel measures a four-hundred-yard run, the torpedo can't explode. But after that, an impact, or even the presence of a steel hull, will cause an explosion. If this torpedo had forced the outer door open, Roger knew, the warhead would be sticking out into the sea ahead of the tube. The question was, how far? Far enough to allow the fateful little paddle wheel to turn when we moved ahead? Far enough to enable him to reach down and jam it so it wouldn't turn? If not, could the torpedo be worked past the bent outer door, or be forced back into the tube?

These were the questions Roger sought to answer as he and Smith gasped, dived, and groped in the black water. The answers were all bad.

The door was sprung open a few inches, with the warhead of the fish hard against it. There was no hope of getting it in or out. It was stuck, and it would remain stuck until we returned to Pearl — or until it fired. As to the safety factor, Roger thought the paddle wheel was not far enough out in the water to be activated.

This hope, that the torpedo would remain harmlessly jammed in the tube, was the best he could report to the captain. He and Smith climbed out of the water at last, we all stood nervously on the bridge talking it over, and finally the captain ordered slow speed ahead. We held our breaths for the first four hundred yards, waiting for an explosion that didn't come. Eventually, as the waiting palled, everyone not on watch decided to go below and die in his bunk.

We didn't know it then, but life with the torpedo in tube six had only begun. It was still there the next day, and the

next, and the next. We couldn't get it out of the tube, and
we couldn't get it back inside the boat. We even opened the
inner door, put a block and tackle on the torpedo, and tried
to pull it in as the sea poured past it into the boat, but it
wouldn't budge.

At first the tension was unbearable. We ate, slept, and
dreamed with the constant fear that the torpedo was going
to arm itself — that it was in fact even that moment in the
final turn of the paddle wheel. On quiet nights, we would
go in little groups to the forward torpedo room and gather
around the wounded tube. Someone would press his ear
against the bronze barrel and report, "It's ticking!" There
would be a nervous snort from the rest of us. "The hell it is.
That's the torpedoman snoring." Weird rites were invented
and performed to appease the gods of the torpedo tube.

You can steel yourself for death only so long. Little by
little, we grew resigned to the threat, and eventually we
even took minor moments of comfort from it. Whatever
else went wrong, we could always say, "Well, it doesn't
matter. That damned torpedo's going to go off pretty soon
anyhow."

Another difficulty helped to divert us from our death
watch. The bow buoyancy vent jammed shut.

The bow buoyancy tank is up in the very bow of the
ship. When you are submerged and ready to surface, you
blow air into it in order to come up in a hurry with a good
up-angle. Conversely, you open the vent when you dive,
and if the vent won't open, you can't get under.

We had noticed for several days that it was getting

harder and harder to open the vent. On the night of September 25, still less than a week after our first attack, it jammed and wouldn't open at all.

This meant we were unable to dive until it was fixed. The hapless Roger Paine and I, along with Andrew Lennox, the chief motor machinist mate, and a couple of auxiliarymen, were named a working party to see what could be done to get us under — and the sooner the better, as daylight was fast approaching. It was a nerve-tingling experience. We had to remove the cover and get down into the tank itself through the small manhole. Inside, the tank was slimy, black, and covered with a greasy anticorrosive coating. Our dim flashlights were useful chiefly in illuminating one another's tense faces. We all knew that, in these enemy waters, any surprise encounter would mean the *Wahoo* had to dive, if it could, whether we were still in the tank or not. I reminded the others that, according to rules of naval etiquette, the senior officer always leaves a compartment first, but Roger silenced me. With my rear end in the opening, he pointed out, we could never vent the tank.

With the bow buoyancy vent, as with the jammed torpedo, we had to settle for an uneasy compromise. The operating mechanism was hopelessly jammed. All we could do was leave the manhole cover off the tank. This meant we could always vent the tank, but we couldn't use it for a quick surface or to check a too-steep angle in going down. It would be hard to come up without bow buoyancy, but it would be impossible to go down with the vent closed. We preferred to go down and then come up the hard way.

* * *

So for the remainder of that patrol, which ended October 17, we operated with a jammed bow buoyancy vent and a torpedo that might annihilate us at any minute. These two mechanical foul-ups seemed to set the tone of the patrol, for within a single week we had to watch a seaplane tender, an aircraft carrier, and two destroyers go past without firing a round at them.

The tender, the *Chiyoda*, was sighted in the daytime, while we were submerged. He was at a range of about twelve thousand yards, headed for Piano Pass, and at first we thought we had him. But while we were trying to close the range, he made three left zigs, and before we could get into position, he disappeared toward Truk.

That was simply bad luck. It made us lick our chops, but there was nothing we could do about it. It was different with the carrier. That was one we all felt we should have had.

In those early days of the war in the Pacific, an aircraft carrier was considered an almost inconceivable prize for a submarine. The best achievements of our subs had been the sinking of the damaged carrier *Soryu* by the *Nautilus* at Midway, and the sinking of a heavy carrier by the ancient but valiant *S-44* on the day after the disastrous Battle of Savo Island that followed the landing of the Marines at Guadalcanal. Now, suddenly, we were looking at the carrier *Ryujo* through our periscope. If we bagged him, it would be the first live, fully commissioned carrier to be sunk by one of our subs. When word went round that the big ship had been spotted, our men were wild with excitement.

This was early on the morning of October 5. We were in the southern part of our patrol sector, some distance southwest of Truk, when the carrier and two destroyers appeared in the periscope, about five and a half miles away, traveling at a speed of fourteen knots. We bore relative from the carrier sixty degrees starboard, which meant that while we were not on courses that converged sharply, we might make it into firing position if we poured on the coal and burned out our batteries.

But we didn't. We closed the range to about seven thousand yards, and then watched him go over the hill untouched. After he got by, we surfaced in the daylight — he was a prize worth taking chances for — and gave chase, but rain squalls forced us to give it up.

It is easy enough to second-guess an affair like this years later, and I have no intention of doing that now. A dozen factors, human or mechanical or both, could have made us lose our prize; it is unimportant now. What is worth noting, I believe, is the effect such a disappointment can have on the men involved. Certainly our loss of the *Ryujo* was one of the most important things, though in a negative sense, that happened to us during the entire patrol. It played havoc with our self-confidence, our faith in our boat, and our aggressiveness in general. We were to live with the memory of it for the remainder of the war. For some of us, I expect, it came to be no more than a memory in time, but others almost certainly were pushed in later months to extremes of indecision or, on the other hand, foolhardiness. In war as in peace, the thing that does not happen is often more important in the long run than many things that do.

Two days later, brooding and discouraged, we left our assigned area and started for home. And now, as if offering us the hope of a later chance to prove ourselves, fate intervened to save our lives.

We were in the vicinity of the Marshalls, out of dangerous waters and traveling on the surface. Roger Paine and I, old friends by now, had the morning watch, the captain was on the bridge, and all seemed serene and peaceful. Our radar, which did not always work, was scanning the sky for planes, or at least we hoped it was, our lookouts were on the alert, and we were secure in the belief that the enemy was far behind. My first warning of danger was the sudden *Ooga! Ooga!* of the diving alarm. Aft on the bridge, I came forward to follow the others down the hatch, and suddenly saw the cause of the alarm.

Ahead of us, low over the water and only half a mile away, came a Mitsubishi 97 bomber. How he had got so close before he was sighted was a question of only academic interest, for clearly we were finished. Bomb bay open and headed straight at us, on he came. He would be over us before I could even shut the hatch. If ever a submarine was doomed, it was the *Wahoo* at that moment.

We dived. It was an empty gesture, even a mistake with the plane so close already, but we followed our reflexes and dived. And as we slipped down into the water for what we knew was to be the last time, we waited for the blast.

Incredibly, it didn't come. Tension mounted unbearably in the control room as the silence lengthened. Then, slowly and fearfully, we began to hope.

We were miles away, running deep, before we could actually believe our good fortune. For some reason utterly beyond explaining, he had not dropped his bomb. Had it stuck? Had he blacked out? Had his hand frozen on the controls at the last moment? Whatever the cause, he had missed the sort of opportunity that comes to a bomber pilot once in a lifetime. Thinking back to the *Ryujo*, we could almost sympathize with him.

So we returned to Pearl, a little ashamed by now of our one small freighter but suddenly happy to be back at all. The *Wahoo* went into drydock, where the outboard door was cut off the number six torpedo tube and it was established that the fateful paddle wheel had made a few turns but not enough to arm our jammed torpedo. And while this and other ills of the *Wahoo* were repaired, its officers went off to the Royal Hawaiian for two weeks of rest and recuperation.

It was already a tradition that when you came in from a patrol, a relief crew went aboard the boat to make repairs and bring it back to fighting trim while the regular crew went ashore and forgot the submarines, the war, and virtually everything else for two weeks. Whoever established the tradition knew what he was doing. It took just about two weeks to get over the strain.

I was doubly glad to be back because my brother John's ship, the cruiser *Minneapolis*, was at Honolulu when we arrived. He was the navigator on the *Minneapolis*, which had been in a night engagement with the enemy off Guadalcanal and had had her bow blown off by a torpedo launched from a Japanese destroyer. They had had a long, painful, and dangerous trip back to Pearl. John was on duty the day we got in, but the next evening he came over to the Royal Hawaiian and we had a royal time, solving all the world's problems, winning the war, and deciding our own futures. There was nothing to show for all this the next morning but a hangover, but we both felt it had been worth it.

I wrote long letters to Ann and Billy, telling them we hoped to do better on our next patrol and assuring them I would probably be home on leave by not later than the following summer.

And I went swimming often in the pool at the submarine base.

One day at the pool I chanced upon another swimmer, and before we knew it, we were competing against one another like two boys from opposite sides of town who happen to meet at the swimming hole. I fancied myself as a swimmer; I had been captain of the swimming team at the Naval Academy and an All-American water-polo player, which admittedly is a pretty empty honor when you consider how few water-polo teams there are in the United States.

But this fellow, a massive, big-handed man who looked to be about my own age, could swim better than I could. After he had proved it thoroughly, we climbed out and got acquainted. His name, which meant nothing to me at the time, was Mush Morton. The "Mush" was short for Mushmouth, a nickname his Kentucky accent had earned him at the Naval Academy.

I met him again when our two weeks were over and the *Wahoo* set out on its second war patrol. Lieutenant Commander Dudley W. Morton, five years my senior, had been assigned to the *Wahoo* as prospective commanding officer, or makey-learn. His job was simply to take a ride with us on a war patrol and observe everything he could so that he would be qualified to command. The system called for commands to go to the senior officers, of course, but sometimes they lacked the combat experience of their juniors. So ships often went out with officers aboard as makey-learns, to pick up the ropes before they assumed command over men more experienced than themselves in warfare in general or in the particular area.

Mush, we learned, was not without combat experience. He had been in command of an R-boat in the Atlantic. The story was that he had come in for a bit of criticism because he had been unable to get his old tub in close enough to shoot at a German U-boat he had sighted. It seemed appropriate that a man who had missed his chance at a U-boat should become makey-learn on a sub that had missed its chance at a carrier.

This time we went directly to the Solomons, where the battle still raged for Guadalcanal. And again we ran head-on into disappointment. Our first two targets got away without a torpedo being fired. Then, on the tenth of December, we sank our second freighter.

It was in a convoy of three, escorted by a destroyer, heavily loaded and headed for the Shortlands area south of Bougainville. The captain concentrated on the destroyer first, but it passed us, making such radical maneuvers that we couldn't get in a good shot, so we picked the largest freighter, one of 8500 tons, and fired a spread of four torpedoes. Three of them hit, and as the destroyer wheeled to the attack, we went down to the depths to take our punishment.

He laid down his first depth-charge pattern across our stern as we were passing 120 feet, going deep. It was worse than our first depth-charging, but easier, too, because we had been through it before. In all, he dropped about forty depth charges on us. Our main induction valve lifted and we took some water, the antenna trunk and the bridge speaker flooded, some lights were knocked out, and various nuts and bolts flew through the air. The only serious trouble came when a gasket on the negative tank inboard vent carried away, the flood valve failed to hold, and we found ourselves dropping below a safe depth. But on the second try, using the negative vent stops and locking the flood valve closed by hand, we came out of it and got back to a reasonable depth.

At sundown we came up to periscope depth in time to see our target sink. One of the other two freighters was standing down the coast, and the other was beyond the target, picking up survivors. The destroyer was still patrolling the area vigorously, and we left without a try at the other freighters.

We were proud to have sunk another target, but the exultation of our first experience was already fading, and of course we made a point of showing even less excitement than we felt. After all, we were veterans now.

These were busy waters we were in. A day or two later we made contact with another enemy ship, but didn't get within firing range. Two days after that we sighted a Japanese hospital ship, headed for the Shortland Islands, and observed one of the mildly ironic refinements of warfare by letting it go past. It was only a few hours later, that same day, that we sank another target and learned a lesson that kept me jittery the rest of the war.

We were still off the south end of Bougainville, near the Shortlands, and I had the periscope watch. Except for the hospital ship, it had been a quiet, uneventful day, and I was taking the usual ten-minute sweep without really expecting to see anything. I had always promised myself that when the fateful day came in which I made my first periscope sighting of the enemy, I would have a very crisp, matter-of-fact report to send to the captain, but what I saw now took me off guard. It was another submarine, on the surface and very close. Subs have to be close to be seen through a periscope, because they are so low in the water. This one was only about three thousand yards away. I gave an incredulous whistle and yelled, "Jesus Christ, call the captain!"

If there ever was a sitting duck, she was it. There she was, a lone submarine completely unaware of our presence, with no reserve buoyancy, no escort, of course, and no great speed. We swung toward her, noting the large Japanese flag and the designation *I-2* on the side of her conning tower, and fired a spread of three torpedoes. The first one hit about twenty feet forward of the conning tower, and in less than a minute the sub went down with some of her crew still visible on the bridge.

It is one thing to sink an orthodox surface vessel, and another to sink a craft just like your own, even if it is manned by the enemy. Before, what we had seen or imagined in our moments of triumph was simply an angular silhouette sinking into the water, as impersonal as a chip on a pond. Now we pictured the men themselves, trapped in tiny compartments like our own as the torpedo hit. In the moment of the explosion, we looked at one another with stiff faces.

About two and a half minutes later came an unexpected climax. Plainly through our hull we could hear a crunching noise, the sound of metal collapsing inwardly. It was easy enough to interpret *that*. Some of the poor devils had got a compartment sealed off in the first seconds after she had been torpedoed, and they had lived a pitiful fraction of time longer in the sealed compartment until the submarine sank deep enough for the water pressure to collapse the compartment.

After that, when the *Wahoo* was on the surface, it had the most alert lookouts in the whole damned Navy. They could, and did, spot floating coconuts on the horizon. Every one of us had been present at a chilling demonstration of the fact that a submarine afloat is in constant danger of being sighted by a submerged submarine and caught while it is almost as helpless as a fish out of water. From that day on, I was never fully at ease on the surface. There is something doubly terrible about being destroyed by one of your own kind.

It was while the sinking of the Japanese sub was still fresh in our minds that we had trouble with our own boat, trouble that could have been serious without the mighty muscles of Morgan, the quartermaster who had waved the .45 at me that far-off night before we left the States.

Like most submarines then in action, the *Wahoo* had two periscopes. The broomstick, a tall, narrow scope with a small tip, was normally used in the conning tower for approaches. The night scope, with a bigger tip to admit more light, was intended for use only in the control room, below the conning tower, and was designed for shallower periscope depths than the broomstick. Early on this patrol, the captain had been provoked by his inability to see a target well during a thunderstorm in which brilliant flashes of lightning occurred at irregular intervals, so he had determined to move the night scope up to the conning tower for better visibility in such cases. To do this, it was necessary to remove a metal plate in the periscope track between the conning tower and the control room, lift out a heavy steel skirt, and bolt it in the control room overhead in place of the plate.

The job was undertaken while we were submerged. The plate was removed, and the *Wahoo* began to leak dangerously. To halt the leak, the skirt had to be lifted promptly and bolted into place, but space, always a major factor on a submarine, complicated the problem. The skirt was extremely heavy, and not more than two men could find room to lift it. Even in the best circumstances they might have been unable to lift it, but in the cramped space they had, it became increasingly clear that they couldn't.

They were heaving and gasping, and the water was pouring in, when Morgan, who had been standing nearby, let out a roar and pushed them aside. Then, by himself, he lifted the skirt into position and held it while it was safely bolted. Crouched there with his muscles bulging and the sweat pouring from his half-naked body, he looked like Atlas holding up the world, and as far as we were concerned, he was. I said earlier that this feat virtually saved the boat. Perhaps that is an exaggeration. We could have stopped the leak, but we would have had to quit our patrol and go back in to get our periscope repaired, and under those circumstances it would have been highly dangerous. At any rate, no one was hesitant at the time about giving Morgan credit for saving the boat. I was glad to see he had decided he liked the Navy after all.

We put into Brisbane on December 26, with two targets to our credit but more discouraged than we had been at the end of the first patrol. The *Wahoo*, which we had lived with from its earliest stages of construction and which we had sworn was going to be a great fighting ship, was not making much of a record, and we knew it. We had excuses: there had been mechanical troubles, and we had to learn by experience, and we had waited in the wrong places at the wrong time like unlucky fishermen; but knowing all this, and even allowing for the fact that our morale had been lowered by the experience of spending Christmas on a submarine, we still felt thoroughly discouraged. We didn't want good excuses; we wanted a good record.

Our first look at Australia didn't make us feel any better. Later we were to learn to love the place and its people, but when we moored alongside the submarine tender *Sperry* in the harbor at Brisbane and went off to seek our rest facilities, we found they were a far cry from the Royal Hawaiian at Honolulu. All the officers except the skipper and the exec were given rooms in a dingy hotel that made the wardroom of the *Wahoo* seem luxurious by comparison. We stood it for a couple of days and then learned that a beach cottage was available at Paradise Beach, a resort spot about fifteen miles from Brisbane. We piled aboard a ridiculous little train that puffed its way out to the beach at irregular intervals, looked the cottage over, and rented it. Most of us spent the remainder of our rest period there.

We had to do our own cooking on a gasoline stove that had a habit of exploding when we tried to light it, but the beach was wonderful. We had it pretty much to ourselves; because of the undertow, only the most enthusiastic swimmers among the Aussies would swim there, and most of that group was off at war. But when you got the knack of it, it was fun. The undertow was parallel to the beach, and you could hop in and be carried along by it for miles. We spent most of our time out there, for lack of anything better to do. I expect it was the healthiest rest period any of us had during the whole war.

We did have some brandy with us, but all it did was demonstrate how situations alter tastes. Back on the *Wahoo*, after a depth-charging or some other strenuous experience, we would occasionally issue a two-ounce bottle of brandy to each member of the crew. Remembering how wonderful it had tasted after a depth-charging, we had resolved that the first chance we got, we were going to take some ashore and really live it up.

Well, we got it off the *Wahoo*, all right. We opened it at the first opportunity, and got all set for a real treat. And the stuff was awful; it almost blistered our throats.

5

Mush the Magnificent

As THE YEAR ENDED, the *Wahoo* was assigned a new captain. Marvin Kennedy, the red-haired perfectionist who had supervised construction, had trained us strenuously and well, and had taken us on two patrols, went on to another assignment, and our makey-learn, big, playful Lieutenant Commander Dudley W. Morton of Kentucky, was put in command. And, in the quiet January days at Brisbane before we put to sea again, we tried to decide what the change would mean.

Everybody liked Mush. He had done a thorough job of getting acquainted with the *Wahoo* and its crew during the second patrol. He was always roaming the narrow quarters, his big hands reaching out to examine equipment, his wide-set eyes missing nothing. He was largely without responsibility on that patrol, and he had been one of the boys. The tiny wardroom always brightened when Mush squeezed his massive shoulders through one of the two narrow doorways and found a place to sit. He was built like a bear, and as playful as a cub. Once he and I got into an impromptu wrestling match after our coffee, and he put a half nelson on me and bore down just a little. Something in the back of my neck popped, and my head listed to port for weeks afterward. Even today it comes back occasionally, and I always think of Mush.

The crew loved him. Submarines are perhaps the most democratic of all military units, because within their cramped confines there simply isn't room for echelons of rank and dignity. Even so, for many officers the transition from camaraderie to authority is a jerky and awkward one, so that their men are never completely at ease. It was not this way with Mush. His authority was built-in and never depended on sudden stiffening of tone or attitude. Whether he was in the control room, swapping tall tales with Rau, the chief of the boat, or wandering restlessly about in his skivvies, talking to the men in the torpedo and engine rooms, he was as relaxed as a baby. The men were not merely ready to follow him, they were eager to.

But there had been times on the second patrol when his casually expressed opinions suggested the absence of any reasonable degree of caution. It is one thing to be aggressive, and another to be foolhardy, and it would be a mistake to think that the average man in submarines was a fire-breathing buccaneer who never thought of his own hide. Most of us, in calculating the risk, threw in a mental note that we were worth more to the Navy alive than dead — and to our wives and children as well. But when Mush expressed himself on tactics, the only risk he recognized was the risk of not sinking enemy tonnage. Talking it over at Paradise Beach, Roger and I were mildly concerned.

Another thing that worried us was that Dick O'Kane, the exec, clearly had no reservations about Mush. The two were in agreement on everything. And we still weren't too sure about Dick. He talked a great deal — reckless, aggressive talk — and it was natural to wonder how much of it was no more than talk. During the second patrol Dick had grown harder to live with, friendly one minute and pulling his rank on his junior officers the next. One day he would be a martinet, and the next he would display an overlenient, what-the-hell attitude that was far from reassuring. With Mush and Dick in the saddle, how would the *Wahoo* fare?

Nevertheless, we looked forward almost eagerly to the prospect. As many a politician has learned, when morale sags, any change is welcome. And our doubts about Mush were theoretical; our reasons to like him were real. I remember writing to Ann about the change in glowing terms.

I wrote, too, about one of those happy meetings that occur sometimes in wars. Ed Blakely, a good friend of ours, turned up at Brisbane shortly before we were to leave, and I was able to pass his good news on to Ann: he and his wife Ginger were expecting a baby the following month. I promised to get her address and pass it on to Ann. That was the last time I saw Ed. He was lost on his next patrol.

The *Wahoo* was ready for sea on January 16, 1943, and even before we left the harbor at Brisbane, the impact of our new skipper was felt. Meals in the wardroom took on the nature of parties; instead of staring at our plates and fretting over our responsibilities, as we had grown accustomed to doing, we found ourselves led along by a captain who was constantly joking, laughing, or planning outrageous exploits against the enemy. Overnight, it seemed, the photographs of Japanese ships that had been pasted all over the *Wahoo*, even in the head, came down — not by order, but through some unspoken understanding that Mush would approve — and in their places went some of the finest pin-up pictures in the U. S. Navy. Identification of silhouettes is a useful occupation, but some silhouettes are more rewarding than others.

Our instructions were to proceed to the Carolines. To this day I don't remember exactly where we were supposed to go, because we never got there. But there was one sentence, almost incidental, in our orders that was to have considerable significance. En route, we were to reconnoiter Wewak harbor.

To reach the Carolines we would sail north from Brisbane and follow the northeast coast of New Guinea upward, past Buna, where General MacArthur's troops were even then driving back the Japanese, and on up along the enemy-held shore. And somewhere along there, reports indicated, was a harbor called Wewak that might hold enemy ships. We were to see what we could find.

If we hurried, Mush decided, we could spend more time there than our operation order had allowed. So as we moved along the New Guinea coast, we stayed on the surface for greater speed. It was a strange and unfamiliar experience to see enemy land lying black and sinister on the port hand, to feel the enemy planes always near us, and yet it was invigorating. Contrary to all tradition on the *Wahoo*, we kept to the surface during daylight hours for six days, submerging only for one quick trim dive each morning, though we were almost never out of sight of land and often within close range of enemy airports.

The *Wahoo*'s combat attitude had changed in other ways. Now, instead of two officers, four lookouts, and the quartermaster on the bridge when we were on the surface, we cruised with only one officer and three lookouts, but somehow we felt we had never been so well guarded. And Mush had removed the bunk previously installed for the skipper in the conning tower. When he was ready for sleep, he went down to his stateroom and slept like a baby, leaving no doubt that the officer of the deck was on his own, that he was trusted, and that he was thoroughly in command unless or until he asked for help.

Only occasionally did Mush intervene. One day he wandered up for a bit of conversation when I was on the bridge, and suddenly as we talked we sighted a plane about eight miles away. About the same time, the radar picked it up and confirmed the range. We had always dived when we sighted a plane in the past, so I turned for the hatch. Mush's big hand landed on the back of my collar just as I reached the ladder.

"Let's wait till he gets in to six miles," he said softly.

I turned and went back. Great Lord, I thought, we're under the command of a madman.

We stood and watched as the plane closed the range. At six and a half miles his course began to take him away from us, and in a few minutes he had faded from sight. By gambling that he hadn't seen us, Mush had saved us hours of submerged travel, but even though it had worked, I wasn't sure I was in favor of it.

Meanwhile, as we neared the area where Wewak should be, the chart problem became acute. Our orders gave no hint of its position and none of our charts of the New Guinea coast showed it by name; it could have been any one of a dozen unnamed spots. How could we reconnoiter a harbor whose location we didn't know?

At first, most of us had considered this only a minor problem. If we didn't know where Wewak was, we didn't know. We could take a look at some of the more promising spots, and make our reports, and be on our way. Then one night in the wardroom a different light was put on the matter. Mush, Dick, Roger, Hank Henderson, and I were looking at the charts, speculating on which tiny dent in the coast might be Wewak, when Mush asked innocently what we understood to be the meaning of the word "reconnoiter."

I may have hammed up the answer a little, but not much.

"Why," I said, "it means we take a cautious look at the area, from far out at sea, through the periscope, submerged."

Mush grinned. "Hell, no," he said. "The only way you can reconnoiter a harbor is to go right into it and see what's there."

Roger and Hank and I looked at each other in sheer consternation. Now it was clear that our captain had advanced from mere rashness to outright foolhardiness. For a submarine, as anybody knew in those days, was a deep-water ship that needed broad oceans and plenty of water under its keel to operate. And harbors are often treacherous at best, even when you enter them in surface ships handled by experienced pilots equipped with the very latest charts. It would be madness for the *Wahoo* to submerge and enter an enemy harbor whose very location on the map we didn't know.

Later, submarines penetrated other harbors, but if any had done so at that time, none of us knew about it, and it was against every tradition that had been built up on the *Wahoo*. Yet here was this skipper of ours, grinning at us under his jutting nose as if he had just told a funny story, assuring us we were going to do it and we'd damned well better find out which harbor was Wewak or he'd just pick the most likely one and go in.

After word of this attitude of Mush's got out, the search for a chart of Wewak harbor increased markedly. And in the end it was Bird-Dog Keeter, the motor machinist's mate who had sighted the *Wahoo*'s first victim, who came to the rescue. I was making a tour through the engine room one night when I found Keeter poring over a book. He looked up, grabbed my arm, and yelled over the roar of the engines:

"Hey, Mr. Grider, is this the Wewak we're going to?"

I grabbed the book out of his hand. It was an Australian high-school geography book he had bought while we were on leave, and he had opened it to a page that showed a map of New Guinea. Sure enough, there on the northeast coast was a tiny spot marked WEWAK.

A couple of months before, the idea of entering an enemy harbor with the help of a high-school geography would have struck me as too ridiculous even to be funny. Now I almost hugged the book and charged forward to the wardroom with it as if it were the key to the destruction of the entire Japanese Navy.

Mush took one look at it and reached for our charts. The wardroom began to hum with activity.

One of our charts did have a spot that seemed to correspond with the latitude and longitude of Wewak as shown in the book, but even then we weren't much better off. On our big chart, the Wewak area covered a space about the size of a calling card — hardly the detail you need for entering a harbor. We were on the track now, though, and Mush's determination to enter Wewak, regardless, made what we had seem a lot better than nothing.

Dick O'Kane and his quartermaster, a man named Krause, took over. First, Krause made a tracing of the area from our chart onto a piece of toilet paper. Next, we took my old Graflex camera and rigged it as an enlarger, using the ship's signal lamp as the projector light. We clamped this rig to the wardroom table and projected the enlarged image onto a large sheet of paper spread on the wardroom deck. Then, with all lights turned out, Dick and Krause traced the projected lines on the new sheet, and we had a chart. It might have made a cartographer shudder, but it was a long way ahead of no chart at all.

What we saw was a rough drawing, not of a harbor, but of a protected roadstead with islands on all four sides. And there was a name for one of the islands: Mushu. In the general triumph, this was taken as a positive omen of good hunting. And as I reassembled my Graflex, I could not help reflecting that it, too, was an omen. It was a camera that

had been used in World War I by my father and his friend
and fellow flier Elliott Springs. My father had been killed
in action, and Elliott had saved the camera and given it to
me as a memento. I had always treasured it as something
special and had got myself named ship's photographer in
order to bring it along on the *Wahoo*. When I thought that
a chart fashioned with the help of an ancient camera used
by my father more than a quarter of a century before on another side of the world in another war would lead us into
Wewak harbor, I too began to believe there was some kind
of guiding destiny behind the *Wahoo*'s third patrol.

So, in the limited time remaining, we planned and discussed and prepared. Every scrap of information we had
been able to get about Wewak was transferred to our chart.
From what we assembled, it appeared that it might be plaus-
ible after all to penetrate the harbor. There was plenty of
room; the harbor was about two miles across in most places,
and we believed the depth might be as much as two hundred
feet in most areas. Mush was delighted. He ignored the un-
certainties and concentrated on the fact that we would have
deep water, if we stayed where it was, and unmistakable
landmarks, if we could spot them in time to use them.

It was summer in that hemisphere, and the sun rose early.
We adjusted our speed to arrive at Wewak just before dawn
on January 24. At three-thirty in the morning, just as the
eastern horizon was beginning to gray, we dived, two and a
half miles off the entrance, and proceeded submerged toward Wewak harbor.

Actually, there were several entrances, but we were sure
of only one. The harbor extended about nine miles in from

this point, making a dogleg that obstructed the view. We approached around the western end of one of the islands to investigate the bay beyond, but before Dick could see anything else, he spotted two torpedo boats in the periscope, headed in our direction. This was no time to be seen by small boats, so we ducked down, waited awhile, and tried again.

This time the torpedo boats were gone. There was a small tug in the distance with a barge alongside, but no other shipping in sight. We poked around into another area, a strait between two of the islands, and Dick saw something that may have been radio masts on the far side of a third island. Mush suggested we go around for a better look, but this time a reef showed up to block our way.

We spent the entire morning nosing around that harbor, trying to find out what was in it and where the safe water was. As Dick spotted light patches of water in the scope, he called off their locations and we noted them on our chart as shallows. From time to time we could pencil in landmarks. One of these we called Coast Watcher Point.

A strong southward current had been complicating our problems ever since we entered the harbor, and it was this current that was responsible for the naming of Coast Watcher Point. It swept us so close to the point that all of us in the conning tower, taking turns at the periscope, could see a Japanese lookout, wearing a white shirt, sitting under a coconut tree right on the point. We saw him so clearly, in fact, that I am sure I would recognize him if I passed him on the street tomorrow.

Except for this chance the rest of us had to look, Dick

O'Kane had made all the periscope observations. Mush had a unique theory: he believed the executive officer, not the captain, should handle the periscope throughout an approach and attack. This, he explained, left the skipper in a better position to interpret all factors involved, do a better conning job, and make decisions more dispassionately. There is no doubt it is an excellent theory, and it worked beautifully for him, but few captains other than Mush ever had such serene faith in a subordinate that they could resist grabbing the scope in moments of crisis.

Right now, Mush was in his element. He was in danger, and he was hot on the trail of the enemy, so he was happy. For all the tension within us, we managed to reflect his mood. The atmosphere in the conning tower would have been more appropriate to a fraternity raiding party than so deadly a reconnaissance. Mush even kept up his joking when we almost ran aground.

This happened because of the dual nature of a periscope. It is a very precise instrument with two powers of magnification: a low power that magnifies objects one and a half times, to give you about the same impression you would get with the naked eye, and a six-power magnification to bring things in very close. So everyone was concerned when, on one of his looks, Dick called from the periscope:

"Captain, I believe we're getting too close to land. I have the periscope in high power, and all I can see is one coconut tree." If only one coconut tree, even magnified six times, filled his scope, then we were dangerously close.

"Dick," said the captain in a tone of mild reproof, "you're in *low* power."

In the electric silence that followed, Dick flipped the handle to high power and took an incredulous look.

"Down periscope!" he yelped. "All back emergency! My God, all I can see is one *coconut!*" We backed away from there in record time.

By early afternoon, Mush was beginning to lose his good humor. We had spent half a day looking for a target worth shooting at, and none had showed up. But we had got a good idea of the harbor, and now we went in farther, to where we could get a good look around the dogleg and down the bight, and there at the very end of the dogleg Dick saw what appeared to be the superstructure of a ship. At first sight, he reported it looked like a freighter or a tender of some sort, at anchor.

"Well, Captain," somebody in the conning tower said, "we've reconnoitered Wewak harbor now. Let's get the hell out of here and report there's a ship in there." We all knew it was a joke, however much we wished it weren't.

"Good God, no," said Mush, coming to life. "We're going to go in and torpedo him."

Dick asked him to come over and help identify the potential target, and the two of them stood there like a couple of schoolboys, peering through the scope each time it was raised, trying to decide what kind of vessel lay ahead. At last they agreed, and Mush looked happily around the conning tower.

"It's a destroyer," he said.

Much has been written about the changes great fighters undergo in battle. It has been said that when General Nathan Bedford Forrest, the great Confederate cavalry officer, went into battle, his face became a deep, mottled red, his voice altered, becoming shrill and high-pitched, and his whole countenance took on a look of indescribable fierceness. Mush Morton changed, too, but in a wholly different way. Joy welled out of him. His voice remained the same, but his eyes lit up with a delight that in its own way was as fearful as Forrest's countenance must have been. Here, we were to realize before the *Wahoo*'s third patrol ended, was a man whose supreme joy was literally to seek out and destroy the enemy. It was to drive him to terrifying magnificence as a submarine commander, to make him a legend within a year, and to lead eventually to his death.

Now, as the rest of us worried about the depth of the water, the pull of the unknown currents, the possibility of reefs between us and our target, he smiled at us again.

"We'll take him by complete surprise," he assured us. "He won't be expecting an enemy submarine in here."

Mush was right about that. Nobody in his right mind would have expected us.

We went to battle stations. The conning tower, already crowded, became even more so. Roger Paine took his post at the Torpedo Data Computor, the mechanical brain mounted in the after corner. Jack Jackson, the communications officer, supervised the two sound operators. As assistant approach officer, I turned over my diving duties to Hank Henderson and crouched near the top of the control-room ladder, manipulating a small device known as an "is-was" — a sort of attack slide rule used in working out distances and directions. There were also two quartermasters, a fire controlman, the helmsman, and a couple of others in the tiny compartment.

Dick made his sightings cautiously, easing the periscope up only far enough to see the tops of the masts of the destroyer. We moved at a speed of only three knots. The sea above us was as calm as glass, a condition that makes periscopes very easy to see. All unnecessary auxiliary motors, including the air conditioning, were shut off now; we were rigged for silent running. Voices dropped to whispers, and perspiration began to drip from our faces as the temperature rose toward the 100-degree mark. We had the element of surprise on our side, and nothing else. We were now six miles inside an uncharted harbor, with land on three sides of us, and in a minute or so the whole harbor would know we were there.

The outer doors on our six forward torpedo tubes were quietly opened. We were approaching the range Mush had decided on, three thousand yards. It was a little long, but it should keep us in deep water.

"Stand by to fire One."

Dick O'Kane, crouched around the periscope barrel, flipped his thumbs up to indicate he wanted the scope raised one last time. The long cylinder snaked up. Dick rode the handles, clapping his eye to the eyepiece as soon as it was clear of the floorboards. He let the scope get about two inches out of water and took a quick look around.

"Down scope." There was an urgency in his whisper that brought tension to the breaking point. "Captain, she's gotten under way, headed out of the harbor. Angle on the bow ten port."

Now our plan to catch this sitting duck was gone a-glimmering. She was not only under way, she was headed almost directly at us. The only reasonable thing to do was to get out. Later, perhaps, we could get a shot at her in deep water. But Mush was in no mood to be reasonable.

"Right full rudder!"

Without a moment's pause, he was shifting to a new plan of attack. Now we would run at right angles to the destroyer's course and fire our stern tubes at her as she passed astern.

The conning tower burst into action. Periscope down . . . Roger twirling knobs on the TDC . . . Mush crouched in the middle of the conning tower, breathing heavily, spinning the disks on the is-was . . . orders being shouted now rather than whispered. The destroyer's speed, increasing as she got under way, could only be guessed at. Roger cranked a reading on the TDC, which would automatically generate the correct angles for the gyros. The ship swung hard to the right. Within one minute we were ready to fire.

"Up periscope. . . . Mark! . . . Target has zigged. . . . Angle on the bow forty starboard." Now the destroyer was heading across our bow. More frantic grinding of knobs, another quick guess at his speed — fifteen knots this time.

"Ready. . . . Stand by to fire. . . . Fire One. . . . Fire Two. . . . Fire Three."

The boat shuddered as the three torpedoes left the forward tubes.

"All ahead standard." The bow had begun to rise under the loss of weight forward.

Steam torpedoes leave a wake as wide as a two-lane high-way and a lot whiter. There was no point now in lowering the periscope, for at that range the enemy could simply look down the wakes to where *x* marked the spot. Dick brought the periscope up to full height and watched. After a couple of centuries, he spoke.

"They're headed for him."

Torpedoes run at about fifty knots, but the interval between firing and hitting seems endless.

"The first one missed astern. . . . The second one missed astern. . . . The third one missed astern."

Groans sounded in the conning tower. We had guessed too low on his speed.

"Get another setup!" There was a fierce urgency in Mush's voice. "Use twenty knots."

"Ready."

"Fire Four!"

Again the boat shuddered, and Dick's eyes remained glued to the scope. And again the news, given to us piece-meal between long pauses, was bad.

"Target turning away."

"Damn!"

"The fourth missed. . . . She's swinging on around. . . . Now she's headed right at us."

The situation had changed drastically. Warned by the wakes of the first three torpedoes, the destroyer had begun a fast, determined turn away from us, continuing it for 270 degrees until now she was headed toward us, ready for revenge. A destroyer is named for its ability to destroy submarines, and this one was coming at us now with a deck full of depth charges. We had fired four of our six forward fish. We had four more in our stern tubes, but it would take too long to swing to fire them, and even longer to reload our forward tubes.

"All right," said Mush. "Get set for a down-the-throat shot."

We had talked about down-the-throats in wardroom bull sessions, but I doubt if any of us had ever seriously expected to be involved in such a shot. It is what the name implies, a shot fired at the target while he is coming directly toward you. No one knew for sure how effective it would be, because as far as I know there was then no case in our submarine records of anyone's having tried it. But it had one obvious virtue, and two staggering disadvantages. On the one hand, you didn't have to know the target's speed if the angle was zero; on the other hand, the target would be at its narrowest, and if you missed, it would be too late to plan anything else. In this particular case, we would be shooting a two-ton torpedo at a craft no more than twenty feet wide, coming toward us at a speed of about thirty knots.

A few minutes before, I had been thinking fatuously what a fine story I would have to tell Ann and Billy on my leave. Now I remembered with relief that I had left my will ashore at the beginning of the patrol.

"Ready." From Roger, at the TDC.

"Stand by to fire."

"Range eighteen hundred."

"Fire Five!"

"Periscope is under water. Bring me up."

Hank had momentarily lost control, under the impact of the firing, and we had dropped below periscope depth with that destroyer boiling down on us. "Bring her up, Hank, boy, bring her up," the skipper called down the hatch. An agonizing wait, then, with Dick clinging to the periscope.

"Captain, we missed him. He's still coming. Getting close."

It is strange how, in such situations, some portion of your mind can occupy itself with coolly impersonal analyses of factors not directly connected with your own hide. I found part of myself marveling at the change that had come over Dick O'Kane since the attack had begun. It was as if, during all the talkative, boastful months before, he had been lost, seeking his true element, and now it was found. He was calm, terse, and utterly cool. My opinion of him underwent a permanent change. It was not the first time I had observed that the conduct of men under fire cannot be predicted accurately from their everyday actions, but it was the most dramatic example I was ever to see of a man transformed under pressure from what seemed almost adolescent petulance to a prime fighting machine.

"Stand by to fire Six."

"When shall I fire, Captain?"

"Wait till she fills four divisions in low power."

"Captain, she already fills eight."

Even Mush was jarred. "Well, for Christ's sake," he yelled, "*fire!*"

"Fire Six!" From Dick. Mush echoed him with, "Take her deep!"

We flooded negative and started down, and I went down the ladder and took over from Hank. I couldn't take her really deep, because we had no idea what the depth of the water there was, and it wouldn't help to strike an uncharted reef. But I took her as far down as I dared, to ninety feet, and we rigged for depth-charge attack.

We were no longer the aggressor. Now our time as well as our torpedoes had run out, and we were helpless to fight back. All we could do was grab on to something and stand by for the final depth-charging of the U.S.S. *Wahoo*. Our time had come, and we waited for the end almost calmly.

The first explosion was loud and close. A couple of light bulbs broke, as they always do on a close explosion, and I remember watching in a detached way as the cork that lined the inside of the *Wahoo*'s hull began to flake off in little pieces.

We waited for the second blast, each man lost within himself, looking at objects rather than at other men, no eyes meeting, as is appropriate for the final moments of life.

And the silence continued. Ten, twenty, thirty seconds, until I looked up and saw other eyes coming into focus, faces taking on expressions of wonderment. It was a voice from the pump room that broke the spell.

"Jeez," it said. "Maybe *we* hit *him!*"

There was something ridiculous, almost hilariously so, about the voice. Up in the conning tower Mush heard it, and laughed.

"Well, by God, maybe we did," he responded, his voice now a roar. "Bring her back up to periscope depth, George."

Almost frantically, we wrestled her back up.

Again, Mush left the scope to Dick. He took a long look. "There she is. Broken in two."

Bedlam broke loose on the *Wahoo*.

I waved to Hank to take over in the control room, grabbed my Graflex, and shot up the ladder. Mush had named me ship's photographer, and I was going to get a shot of that target one way or another.

It wasn't easy. Even Mush wanted to take a look at this, and every man in the crowded conning tower was fighting for a turn by the time the skipper turned aside. But at last my chance came.

The destroyer was almost beam to, broken in two like a matchstick, her bow already settling. Apparently, her skipper had lost his nerve when he saw our last torpedo heading toward him and put the rudder over to try to miss it, and by swinging himself broadside to it he had signed the destroyer's death warrant. Now, as she began to sink, her crew swarmed over her, hundreds of men, in the rigging, in the superstructure, all over her decks. As we struggled for positions at the periscope, some of the destroyer's crew returned to their places at the forward deck gun and began firing at our periscope. They continued it as she sank slowly beneath the waves.

Somehow I got a few pictures and moved out of the way. And now Mush, who was almost a tyrant when it came to imposing his will on us in emergencies, returned to the democratic spirit he always showed when something good happened. "Let everybody come up and take a look," he called.

The whole crew came up by turns, overflowing every inch of the control room and the conning tower, each man shoving his way to the scope and bracing himself there for a long, unbelieving look before turning away with whatever word represented the extreme limit of his vocabulary. I heard some remarkable expletives that day.

We were still celebrating when a bomb went off close aboard, and it dawned on us that there was a long way to go before we were out of the woods. Down we went again to ninety feet, realizing there was an airplane up there on lookout for us, and started to pick our way out.

In a moment we began to hear the propellers of small boats, buzzing around the water above us like waterbugs as they searched for us, and we realized the only way to get out of Wewak harbor safely was to keep our periscope down. In addition to the unknowns of current and depth, we had another unknown. Now we must run silent, which meant even the gyrocompass had to be turned off. The only compass we could use was the magnetic compass, never too reliable inside all that steel. We had to make four miles, take a turn to the right, and go about two more miles before we got to the open sea, and if we turned too soon, we were going to run into the island where we had seen the coast watcher sitting under the coconut tree. If we didn't turn soon enough, we were going to hit the reef ahead.

On the way down the dogleg before the attack, I had noticed a young sailor on the sound equipment, listening with great intensity, though he wasn't particularly needed at the time. Now he spoke to Mush.

"Captain," he said, "as we were coming in, I could hear

beach noises on that island. I think I can tell from them when it's abeam."

None of us in the conning tower knew exactly what beach noises were. Since then, I have read that oceanographers say all sorts of things, particularly shrimp, make noises in the ocean, and shrimp in large beds are common in shallow water in that area. Whatever it was, if the man on the sound gear thought he could help, we were ready to listen.

So, relying on him, we prepared for our turn. We waited until he reported the sounds were abaft the beam, then we made our turn, holding our breaths and hoping, and it worked.

We surfaced after dark, about two miles outside the harbor, and looked back. The Japanese had built bonfires on almost every point, on the shore and on the islands, all along the roadstead. They must have been sure we were still in there, and waiting for us to surface. I have always been grateful, mistakenly or otherwise, to the shrimp along Mushu Island and Coast Watcher Point for getting us safely out after our reconnoitering of Wewak harbor.

6
Clean Sweep

Two small islands lie well off the coast from Wewak, forming a natural gateway for inbound shipping. Mush ordered a nightlong crisscross patrol of this area, in hopes of flushing a convoy from Palau, and went below to compose a radio report on the Wewak engagement.

Few duties are as delightful and yet as challenging for a submarine skipper in wartime as that of drafting a report of a successful engagement. It must be brief and factual, but it should be spiced with color and a dash of bravado. A neat turn of phrase is especially to be desired, for it will be read by others than the command to which it is directed. Classmates on other subs within radio range will shortly be decoding it and passing it around their wardrooms, where every word will be analyzed for literary as well as military content. And, in that first fine flush of victory, there are the newspapers and the history books to be considered, and the long tradition of terse, crackling epigrams that adorn the

nation's naval records. It is a dull and unimaginative skipper
indeed who does not expend volumes of creative effort on a
message beneath whose studied nonchalance and modest
gallantry can be read the sterling quality of both boat and
crew.

Mush got off his report, the night passed without enemy
contact, and early in the morning we passed between the
two islands, went ahead at two-engine speed, and set our
base course for Palau. And now, before resuming our mission of destruction, we were given the opportunity to remember our humanity.

I had begun growing a mustache shortly after we left
Brisbane, on an ingenious theory that was shortly to be
tested, and I was standing the four-to-eight watch and fin-
gering my mustache when something showed on the horizon. We had been unusually alert on the bridge that morning despite the inevitable letup after an engagement, not
so much from any sense of danger as from a growing com-
petitive spirit. A young quartermaster named Alfred Simonetti stood watches with me, a soft-spoken, dreamy lad
who took considerable pride in his ability as a lookout,
and a sort of contest had developed between us over who
could be first to spot any object in the water. So when I
was first to sight the stick of a small fishing boat, I sang out
with as much pride as if it had been an aircraft carrier.

We manned the small-caliber deck guns and approached
it cautiously, firing a Tommy gun across the bow when we
got within range just to warn them that we meant business.
But as we drew nearer, our suspicion turned to sympathy.
It was a single-masted schooner-type fishing boat, only

about twenty feet long, and well out from any land, and its crew of six were weak, frightened, and obviously half starved.

None of them could speak English, so we sent for our Filipino mess attendant, Juan Oro Jayson, who tried his inscrutable, respectful best and failed. Next we tried our Chamoro mess attendant, Mona Lisa. Jesus Chargulaf Manalisay had been with us only since we left Brisbane and had already acquired a reputation for laziness, but no one doubted his grasp of his own language. He, too, failed, and we settled for communication by sign language.

The best we could determine, they were Malays. Their engine had gone bad, the weather was flat calm, and they had been adrift for a long time without food or water. There had been nine of them originally, but three had died already; one of those remaining was blind and two others showed all the signs of scurvy. So the war, or our part of it, waited while we hauled out everything we could spare — bread, water, canned goods, cigarettes — and passed it over to our little brown brothers in the fishing boat. We left them with enough supplies for two or three weeks. As we pulled away, one of them rose painfully for a gesture I had always thought was born in the American prize-fight ring: the overhead handshake. Somehow it emphasized the world's smallness and interdependence more than anything else he could have done.

In the afternoon we crossed the equator and my mustache failed me.

We had crossed the line on our second patrol but without appropriate ceremony, much to the disappointment of some of our more seasoned seamen, Chief Torpedoman Russell Rau among them. Rau, who as chief of the boat occupied a position more exalted than that of any top sergeant, had been in the Navy more than twenty years, and he took great satisfaction in the traditional induction of Polliwogs, officers and enlisted men alike, into the mysteries of the Court of King Neptune. He presided over these occasions, as I was to learn, with a vast dignity that even his monstrous, bulging belly failed to lessen.

Perhaps I have an exaggerated memory of the size of that belly. It was well greased with lard and lampblack, and before the day was over, I had to kiss it.

In Brisbane, Mush had promised a full-scale crossing-the-line ceremony if conditions permitted. As one of the prospective initiates, I had been preparing a bit of strategy. I knew the ceremony would be rough, especially on the officers, and at that time I thought, in my foolishness, that by the end of the patrol I would be going home on leave, and I didn't want anything to happen that would mar my appearance. In short, I was afraid they would shave my head. So I had grown a mustache as a sort of burnt offering for the occasion.

We submerged for the big event, and all Polliwogs were herded into the forward battery. As the top-ranking Polliwog (Mush and Dick O'Kane having survived earlier initiations), I was taken first. They blindfolded me and took me through the usual indignities associated with such affairs — the eating of some vile concoction, the electric shock, the kissing of Rau's buttered belly — and then they sat me in a chair and I could hear the buzz of hair clippers. It was the moment I had planned for so craftily. I delivered my line with great feeling.

"Cut off my hair if you want," I begged, "but don't touch my mustache. Please don't touch my mustache!"

The evil of some men is almost too much to believe. They did exactly what I asked. I have had my doubts about that story of Br'er Rabbit and the brier patch ever since.

The *Wahoo*'s greatest day dawned warm and clear. Simonetti and I, feeling the breeze on our exposed skulls as we stood watch, agreed that it had been a rough night for Polliwogs but that we would have plenty of time to relax en route to our station. The watch was almost over. I was wondering what we would have for breakfast as I swept the horizon with the binoculars and stopped at a plume of distant smoke over the horizon.

Smoke was a thing the submariners learned to love during the war. The great weakness of the Japanese merchant marine was that its ships could never stop making smoke. Almost every time we sighted them it was from the smoke they made — a tremendous advantage, for it meant that a ship completely out of sight over the horizon and traveling a course that would not have brought it closer could be spotted, hunted down, and sunk.

Mush came up and we began tracking on the surface. As yet we had no idea what game we were stalking, but none of us doubted we would get it. Wewak had done that for us.

Speed and course were adjusted to get us ahead of the target, and we settled down to speculating whether the smoke came from one ship or two. At last we decided there were two. Sure enough, forty-five minutes later, as we pulled into position well ahead of the enemy's course, the masts of two ships appeared on the horizon. We opened the main ballast-tank vents, slipped under the water, and lay there waiting for them.

There was something unusual about the situation. They were on a course that led nowhere, and they were making ten knots and not even zigzagging. They appeared to be large freighters; they were without an escort; and the nearest land was a couple of hundred miles away. Talking it over, we decided they were expecting the destroyer we had sunk in Wewak to meet them and escort them into New Guinea.

If that was it, Mush's daring, two days before, was paying off again, for they were wholly unprepared for an attack in these waters. Filled with a sort of grim glee, we began our approach.

Our plan was to get to a position about a thousand yards off the track and wait until the first freighter passed. With it on our starboard bow and the second on our port bow, we could fire the first three torpedoes with right gyro angles, quickly shift the last three to left gyro angles, and get both targets. But this kind of approach requires an exquisite nicety of timing, and we overestimated the target speed as we stalked into position, using only the briefest of periscope glimpses. Suddenly we realized we were going to be too close; our torpedoes wouldn't have enough distance to arm themselves before they hit. We would have to get farther away, and in a hurry. So at the last minute, as so often happens, the carefully laid plans were replaced by a hasty substitute: we would turn around, start away from them, and fire our stern tubes. And since the stern had only four tubes, this meant two less chances for a hit.

It took eleven minutes to put the new plan into effect. Then, with Dick working coolly and with incredible speed at the periscope, we fired two fish at the leading ship, got a new setup in seventeen seconds, and let the other two go at the second ship, swinging around the moment the fourth torpedo was gone so we could bring our bow tubes to bear.

It had been done too fast for top accuracy. In the few seconds that marked the change of targets, there simply wasn't time enough for the gyro-setting angle indicator and regulator to catch up with the new setup cranked into the TDC for the third shot. So, while the first two torpedoes hit their points of aim in bow and stern, the third one passed ahead of the second target. But the fourth hit him.

Three hits out of four! There was great joy in the conning tower as we lowered the periscope to complete the turn. It continued for four minutes; then Dick jammed his eye to the scope again, rode it up, and reported the situation.

"There's the first one. . . . She's listing to starboard and sinking by the stern. . . . Mark, here's the other one — she's headed for us, but coming slow. Mark. . . . Here's a ship, angle on the bow ninety starboard, range eighteen hundred."

I remember a feeling of annoyance at Dick's words — annoyance at him, not at the prospect of another target. For, while he had distinctly mentioned three ships, all of us knew there were only two up there.

But three there were. We were entering the sort of situation in which Mush was at his absolute best — a cloudy and confused situation, that is. Here was an injured ship headed directly at us, evidently intent on ramming us, while astern of him and still on the original course was yet another — a big one, Dick added now, maybe a transport.

"Let's get him next," Mush said.

So, while the second ship came steadily at us, we remained at periscope depth, got a quick setup on the third, and fired three of our bow tubes. Not until he could report that two of the torpedoes had hit, did Dick turn the periscope back to our counterattacker. He was still coming, yawing somewhat, but quite close.

"Down the throat?"

"Down the throat?"

There was no point in mastering a new technique, Mush obviously thought, if you didn't keep in practice.

We fired two shots at him from the bow tubes. One of them hit, but he kept right on coming. Before the day ended, I was to have a higher regard for the captain of that freighter than for any other enemy skipper we ever fought.

He almost rammed our conning tower. We got down just in time, went to a hundred feet, turned hard left, and avoided him.

And now that we were sightless, bedlam broke out in the waters around us. Explosions sounded from all directions. They may have been depth charges, or they may have been boiler explosions; we never knew. There was nothing the *Wahoo* could do, anyhow, but stay down, lurching and shuddering, until her tubes were reloaded — and one of them had to remain empty. We had already expended all but nine of our torpedoes.

Eight minutes later Mush brought us back to periscope depth. Our first target had sunk. The second — the one that had almost rammed us — was still going, but very slowly and with evident steering trouble. The third, and it was a troop transport just as Dick had speculated, was stopped dead but still afloat.

"Let's finish him off." There was a fierce joyousness in Mush's command that would have chilled any of us if we had been onlookers rather than participants.

Now began one of the most delicate, excruciating, and ruthless of all the duties a submariner is called upon to perform: the maneuvering for a killer shot at a wounded foe. For all the explosions that had rocked the waters a few minutes before, the sea was now calm again, the top of our periscope glittered in the midday sun, and through its eye Dick O'Kane watched our victims watching us.

They were not idle. It was a big transport, crawling with troops, and they were firing desperately at the periscope with everything they had, rifles and machine guns as well as deck guns, hoping if nothing else to blind us and escape as Ulysses had escaped from Cyclops. Thus far, they had failed.

We came in to a range of a thousand yards, took careful aim, and fired. Dick kept his face jammed against the periscope as though he were trying to climb through it.

"There it goes. . . . It's headed right for him. . . . They're shooting at it. . . . It's going straight at him. . . . It's going under. . . ."

A long silence in the conning tower, and in the water around us.

"Oh, hell!" It was all he needed to say. The torpedo had failed to explode.

"Stand by to fire another!" Mush was momentarily furious. "Same setup!"

"Fire!"

This time, as Dick continued a blow-by-blow account almost identical with his last one, we all heard the telltale click that is the first sign of an exploding warhead. Then came the roar, with Dick's voice riding high and triumphant above it.

"*There she goes!* God damn, what a hit!"

The fish had hit her right under her stack, blowing her midships section sky high, and she had begun a majestic, terrifying roll as I fought my way past the others in the fire-control party to get photographs through the periscope. The soldiers were pouring off her sides, jumping, rolling, falling, and slipping. Then, only seconds after the explosion, her stern shot up into the air, her bow pointed under, and she sank.

Mush allowed only a minute's delay while Roger, Hank, and the others crowded around for a look. Then, relentlessly, he turned the *Wahoo's* nose toward the one ship remaining afloat, the cripple that had tried to ram us.

She was staggering off on an easterly course, hit twice now and able to make no more than about six knots, but not giving up for a minute. Clearly, she had an indomitable captain herself, and he was bent on saving her one way or another. And, at least for the present, he did. Our battery was getting dangerously low — we had been down since eight o'clock, most of the time running at high speed, and it was now a little past eleven thirty — and inch by inch, so slowly that at first Mush refused to believe it was happening, the Japanese skipper pulled his crippled freighter out of our reach.

We were still following when Dick called out fresh news. The masts of a fourth ship had appeared on the horizon, to the right of the cripple.

"Looks like a light cruiser, Captain."

Mush's good spirits came back in a rush. Maybe she was heading for the wreckage of the transport. Our score for the day thus far was a freighter and a troop transport sunk and another freighter damaged; it would be great to add a cruiser to the list. Mush's fierce glee swept the conning tower as the stranger grew larger in our periscope. Then, when she was about five miles away, she turned abruptly to join the cripple, and as she turned, Dick spoke.

"See her better now, Captain. She's not a cruiser, she's a tanker."

Together, and with maddening slowness, the two disappeared over the horizon. Mush cursed philosophically, swung the *Wahoo* around, and brought her to the surface to resume the chase afloat at a higher speed while we charged our batteries.

We were still near the site of the transport's sinking, and we surfaced in a sea of Japanese. They were on every piece of flotsam, every broken stick, in lifeboats, everywhere, and as we cruised among them, they looked at us with expressions beyond description. There were about twenty boats of every type in the water, from large scows down to little rowboats. The water was so thick with enemy soldiers that it was literally impossible to cruise through them without pushing them aside like driftwood. These were troops we knew had been bound for New Guinea, to fight and kill our own men, and Mush, whose overwhelming biological hatred of the enemy we were only now beginning to sense, looked about him with exultation at the carnage.

Combat works its changes in men with chilling speed. It was to be months before I or any others on the *Wahoo* thought to contrast this scene with that of the previous morning, when we had been lavishing supplies and good-will on a handful of wretched men in a becalmed fishing boat.

It was during these nightmarish minutes that Lindhe, our great procurer during the days the *Wahoo* was being built at Mare Island, suffered his greatest ordeal as pharmacist's mate.

The 20-millimeter gun forward of the bridge had been manned when we surfaced, and the crew was handling am-munition sent up from below, when there was a sudden explosion and a sharp cry of pain. A young sailor named Whipp had dropped a shell and it had exploded inches from his foot, almost tearing off his middle toe. He was carried below to Lindhe, the man who was master of all occasions save the one he was trained for. I saw the two of them an hour or so later, after Lindhe had finally driven himself to perform the amputation. He was pale and drawn, and as he tried to describe the operation to me, tears actually came into his eyes. Behind him hobbled young Whipp, looking a little pale himself, but smiling stoically and obviously feeling very, very sorry for poor Lindhe.

We turned to the east at last, bent on four engines flank speed, and ran the periscope far up into the air above us in an effort to locate the freighter and tanker that had escaped us. It was about noon by now, and we were bone-tired, hungry, and emotionally exhausted. As the *Wahoo* raced for new game, we began drifting away as we could be spared to get a little food and hot coffee.

By three thirty, we had sighted the telltale smoke of our targets on the port bow and changed course to intercept. We followed the classic submarine maneuver known as the end-around, closing until we could see the tops of their masts, figuring out their course, and, with our superior surface speed, racing ahead of them so we could at last turn toward them, go under, and wait.

It is not as simple a procedure as it sounds. It requires calculations of relative courses and relative speeds, and it takes a long time, because the difference in speeds is not great. But about five thirty, half an hour before sunset, we were ready to dive again. The tanker and the crippled freighter had us dead ahead and didn't know it.

For all their ignorance of our location, however, they were taking no chances. They were zigzagging frantically. These were two targets that didn't intend to let a submarine wait quietly until they came into range. We had to maneuver at a higher speed than the *Wahoo* had ever made submerged before in order to get into position for a shot.

Mush chose the tanker, as the undamaged target. At six

thirty, when it was already too dark to see anything but a blob through the scope, we fired three bow torpedoes at her, the range about a mile.

One of them hit, and Mush instantly began swinging to line up the stern tubes at the freighter. By now we had only four torpedoes left, all in the stern. From now on our bow would be harmless.

The captain of the crippled freighter was still as alert as ever. Before we could get into position, he turned sharply away. At this rate, we would never complete an approach on him in the dark, submerged, so Mush gave the order to surface.

The tanker, to our surprise, was still going, and on the freighter's quarter. If the two targets had taken off on opposite courses, one would have escaped, because the night was dark and the moon would not rise for about three hours yet. But, to Mush's great delight, they stuck together.

Our problem now was to choose a target, get close on the surface, point our stern at it, and fire. The freighter was firing at us with his deck guns whenever he saw us, even though he couldn't see well enough to do any damage, so we turned our attention to the tanker, whose guns were silent.

The problem of hitting a zigzagging ship is a hard one at best, but when you have to fire at him with your stern tubes, it becomes almost ludicrous. For an hour and a half we tried everything in the book, even backing in on him, a move that failed because when we tried high speed in reverse, the rudder would be forced hard over and we would circle. But Mush was not to be defeated. Watching intently through the darkness, he decided he had diagnosed the tanker's zigzag pattern.

She was making right-angle zigs by now, and Mush kept directly on course the next time the tanker, directly ahead, turned 90 degrees. Sure enough, in a few minutes she zigged back 90 degrees left, and we were parallel and about a mile apart. We pulled in a little, turned left full rudder, and fired two of our stern tubes at her at a range of 1850 yards.

The second one hit her just aft of midships and broke her in two. She sank almost instantly.

That made three down and one to go: the crippled freighter that had been eluding us since early morning. We had been working for twelve hours now — destruction can be very hard work, whatever else it is — and we had only two torpedoes left. But even before the tanker was hit, Mush had given the order to change course and head for the freighter.

The change of course gave us an opportunity to measure the big tanker as she was sinking. She was a huge one, five hundred feet long. We could determine this accurately by the field she filled in the binoculars as we passed at a range of 1250 yards just before she went under.

While Mush had been relentlessly stalking his prey on the bridge, the fire-control party in the conning tower had been growing more and more informal. We had been at battle stations too long to do otherwise. At quiet moments, we would drop below for coffee. As bearings were shouted down from the bridge, Roger would make minor corrections in the data computer, but we were doing little else. The thinking was being left to the mechanical brain built into the computer. The after torpedoes had been ready for firing so long now that no one in the fire-control party was sure there was anyone in the after torpedo room. We had the proper switches thrown, and we knew in a general way that the range to the cripple was fairly long. Beyond that, we were leaving the duel to Mush and the captain of the cripple.

That worthy adversary had plenty of fight left in him. As he ran, he fired, and the fact that the shells came near us now and then in that murky darkness was evidence of the excellence of his gun crew. Up on the bridge, Mush shouted insults into the night as the shells fell. Then, suddenly, the gun crew got our range.

It was disconcerting. They had a flashless powder superior to what we had at the time, and the first indication we had that they were zeroing in was when a shell landed almost on the bridge. We could hear it from the conning tower, ricocheting over Mush's head. Down the hatch he came, grinning in momentary admiration at the job the freighter was doing, and we dived. It was another measure of the cripple's prowess that he could chase a sub — especially Mush's sub — beneath the water in the middle of a moonless night.

We stayed below and followed at a discreet distance until the sound of the splashes ended. Then, fifteen minutes after diving, we came up again and resumed the chase.

There is no room for sentiment in conflict. Valiant or not, he was the enemy and our mission was to sink him. In later years we might be able to think back on that skipper and wish, almost impersonally, that he had made good his escape. But on this night, our job was to dog his tracks and wait for him to make a fatal error. And at last he did.

When he did, it was because the sudden promise of rescue blinded him. He had been zigzagging frantically, on a pattern too changeable for us to solve, when a searchlight suddenly stabbed the sky. It came from far off on the horizon, but even from that distance it was big and bright, and it swept the waters with an air of supreme authority. A destroyer, no doubt, coming to the rescue. And seeing that brilliant ray of hope in the sky, the skipper of the freighter made his one mortal mistake of the long day. He gave up his zigzagging and fled straight for the searchlight.

As fast as he turned, Mush was faster. The instant he saw the light he swung the *Wahoo* directly to it, gambling on the cripple's imprudence. And in those two decisions, made quickly and irrevocably by two men out of sight of one another on a darkened ocean, the doom of one was sealed.

The *Wahoo* won the race, getting between the searchlight and the target and then turning off the course, its stern tubes pointing directly at the path the freighter must take. Three minutes after we stopped and steadied, Mush gave the order to fire our last torpedoes.

The finale caught the fire-control party off guard. The conning tower was empty except for Roger and me when Mush shouted his order to fire. We looked at each other in surprise. Roger leaped to his feet, hit the firing button, manipulated the switches, waited, and hit the button again. Somewhat to our surprise, we felt the boat shudder and knew that the two fish were on their way.

It was a moment I will never forget. We were too tired

to care what had happened, the range was long, and the setup was not too accurate. Besides, we had had all the luck we were entitled to that day. As we waited, I took out a package of cigarettes and offered them to Roger. He took one. The seconds ticked on without any sound from the waters outside. I took a cigarette, pulled out a match, and lit Roger's and mine. Then I exhaled and spoke with grave formality.

"Lieutenant Paine," I said, "if either one of those torpedoes hits, I will kiss your royal ass."

Boom!

Boom!

Exulting on the bridge at his final victory over an enemy it had taken four hits from three separate attacks to sink, Mush missed the most unusual ceremony ever performed in the conning tower of the mighty *Wahoo*.

7

Hail and Farewell

THE ESCORT whose belated arrival had spelled destruction for the cripple was boiling toward us over the horizon. If even one torpedo had remained aboard the *Wahoo*, Mush undoubtedly would have pulled the plug and begun maneuvering for a shot. But we were virtually harmless now, with no armament but our deck guns and small arms, and even our fire-eating skipper was satisfied — or so we thought at the time. We stayed just long enough to see the destroyer's searchlight sweep a clear horizon, and then Mush spoke the magic words:

"Let's head for the barn, boys."

A submarine has several speeds. There is all ahead one third, all ahead two thirds, all ahead standard, all ahead full, and all ahead flank. But the fastest of all is yet another speed, all ahead Pearl Harbor, and this was the speed we set ourselves now. We had plenty of fuel, no torpedoes, and nowhere to go but home. We had sunk a destroyer, two freighters, a troop transport, and a tanker before even reaching our patrol station. Amid the general hilarity, Mush headed for the wardroom to compose a message worthy of the occasion.

It was a beauty. "IN TEN HOUR RUNNING GUN AND TORPEDO BATTLE DESTROYED ENTIRE CONVOY OF TWO FREIGHTERS ONE TRANSPORT ONE TANKER," it said in part. "ALL TORPEDOES EXPENDED." Mush passed it around, and we all agreed the phrase "running gun and torpedo battle" was especially fine. He sent it off to Vice Admiral C. A. Lockwood, Jr., Commander Submarine Force, Pacific Fleet, and Admiral Lockwood came back with a memorable message of his own. As I recall, it went: "COME ON HOME, MUSH. YOUR PICTURE'S ON THE PIANO." In the few hours I had before going on watch at 4 A.M., I slept like a baby, after vainly trying to stay awake long enough to compose some heroic phrases of my own for the letter I would write to Ann.

And then, the next morning, history repeated itself. Again Simonetti and I were on the bridge, joking one another about our ability as lookouts, and again the dawn came up like thunder — and again, in the same direction as before, a familiar smudge of black smoke appeared on the horizon.

"We can't do anything about it this time," I told Simonetti, "but I'll call the captain. Might as well let him see what's going on."

So Mush came up to the bridge and we began tracking the smoke, changing course so we could intercept whatever it was and get a good contact report that might be useful to other submarines in the area. This time the masts of three ships came over the horizon before we dived.

We took turns at the scope, watching as they chugged past. It is a peculiar feeling to see a convoy go by, especially one that appears to be unescorted, without being able to do a thing about it. To the rest of us, with the promise of Pearl bright in our minds, warlike regret was tempered by private relief that this would mean no delay in our return, but to Mush it was unbearable. His implacable hatred of the enemy, a hatred that was all the more chilling for the veneer of good nature that covered it, simply would not let him ignore such a challenge. It was as if this convoy were taunting him, daring him to try something. And as he peered through the scope, a plan was born in the Morton mind.

"Look, fellows," he said softly. "See that little tanker at the stern?"

He waited while we all looked.

"You notice it doesn't have a deck gun?"

He was right. It was the only one of the three ships without armament.

"Looks like it can't make as much speed as the others, too, doesn't it?" Again, like small boys reciting their part of some strange litany, we agreed.

Mush became suddenly brisk. "All right, here's what we'll do. We'll let them go by, and then we'll surface astern of the tanker. That'll scare hell out of all of them, and they'll begin to run. When they do, they're going to run off and leave that little tanker, and then we'll go up alongside and sink it with our deck guns."

All of us voted against the idea, even Dick. But Mush wouldn't be talked out of it. The plan was put into operation.

And it worked just the way he said it would, up to a point. We waited for the ships to go by, and then we surfaced and went charging after them in a threatening manner, and sure enough, the size of the smoke columns doubled, sparks began to fly out of the stacks, and they all took off at full speed toward a rain squall on the horizon. We gave hot chase, not using full speed because we wanted to stay out of their gun range until the little tanker had dropped astern. And exactly according to script, the tanker began to fall farther and farther behind until finally it was out of gun range of the other ships.

"Man the deck guns!" Mush roared triumphantly. "All ahead full!"

The other two ships were disappearing into the rain squall. The deck of the *Wahoo* was suddenly alive with activity. And then, without warning, something appeared *from* the rain squall. It was a destroyer, and it was coming right at us.

I say it was a destroyer because all of us but Mush agreed that it was. He wouldn't admit it. He insisted it was a *chidori*, a miniature destroyer reputed to have no more speed than we could muster.

If Mush was right, we might outrun it. We might even circle back and get the tanker after all. So the *Wahoo* turned and began to run as fast as it could.

If Mush was wrong, if it was a destroyer, we couldn't possibly outrun it, of course. We would be chased under and depth-charged. Being more of a pessimist than our skipper, I went quietly down to the control room, where I could be handy for my duties as diving officer when the alarm sounded.

There is a microphone on the bridge, and everything that is said up there can be heard in the control room. It was a memorable experience to stand and listen to Mush changing his mind. Our radar was out of commission, and the enemy vessel was coming directly toward us, so no one had an accurate idea of the range. At first Mush was utterly confident. "Oh, we're going away from him, we're going away!" he chanted. "That thing can't catch us!" There was a pause then, and we heard the voice of Hank Henderson, the officer of the deck: "Captain, it looks to me like he's getting closer." There was just a trace of doubt in the skipper's voice as he answered. "Oh, hell, Hank, we're gaining on him. He's nothing but an antiquated coal-burning corvette."

We were traveling at flank speed. Under emergency conditions, a submarine's engines are capable of a brief, prodigious outburst of power. The pit log, the indicator that showed our speed, stood at about eighteen and a half knots, which was a very good speed indeed for a submarine that had been out as long as we had. Still, I got on the phone, called back to the maneuvering room, where the speed of the engines is controlled, and talked to the chief electrician's mate.

"Jesser," I said, "are we making all the power we can possibly make?"

He sounded a little hurt. "Yes, sir. I thought you'd be

proud of us. We're making over a hundred per cent power back here."

"Well, you'd damned well better be, because there's a Jap destroyer two miles astern."

The phone clicked and I turned to the pit log. It shot up to twenty-one knots, a record that probably still stands.

Meanwhile, Mush's running comments continued on the bridge. "He can't catch us," he was saying. "We're gaining on him." There was a doubtful grunt from Hank, and another pause, and Mush called out, "Look! He's turning away!"

In reality, as we learned later from Hank, the destroyer had got us into a nice, comfortable range and was turning to bring all his batteries to bear at once. The first hint we had of this below was a sudden interruption in Mush's chant.

"Jesus Christ!" he yelled, his voice rising a full octave. "He's *shooting* at us!"

A second later we heard the splash of shells and the whine of one going directly over the bridge. Now Mush's voice sounded again, on a note of almost comic urgency. "Where's that diving alarm?" he was shouting. "Where's that damned diving alarm?"

As captain, he didn't stand watches, of course, and he had never grown familiar with the location of the button that sounded the diving alarm. I yelled up the hatch to him, "Come on down, Captain," and opened the vents as he swarmed down the ladder, and down we went.

The destroyer (even Mush was willing to admit now that it was one) came over and gave us a depth-charging that was loud and disturbing but did no real damage. Apparently the chase had taken him so far from the ships he was escorting that he decided to hurry on back. At any rate, we got out of it without any real pain, and after a couple of hours a very chastened *Wahoo* surfaced and proceeded toward Pearl Harbor.

Mush knew a ridiculous situation when he saw one. That night he sent Admiral Lockwood another dispatch. "ANOTHER RUNNING GUN BATTLE TODAY," he reported, "DESTROYER GUNNING, WAHOO RUNNING."

We had only one more opportunity to get into trouble before we reached Pearl, and Mush did his best to take advantage of it.

The next day we sighted Fais Island, an enemy outpost boasting some phosphate works, a warehouse, and a refinery, and our skipper decided to see what he could do about it. He was able to confirm the information about Fais on our charts, but that was about all. We did submerge and go in very close to shore, where Dick spotted a nice-looking target at anchor, but we were too close to the beach for even Mush to think of surfacing to gun him. Also, the target had a deck gun of its own.

Thwarted in this, Mush decided to stay around until nightfall and shell the phosphate works with our trusty four-inch gun after dark, shooting over the top of the island from the side away from town. But even this plan was blocked by the appearance of an interisland steamer with a gun mount that arrived in our general area and stayed there. All of us talking together finally convinced Mush that the *Wahoo* had done its duty and that the best plan now was to go on back and get some more torpedoes.

So at last he called it quits for the patrol, and we headed for Pearl with all the speed a crew eager for leave could coax out of the *Wahoo.*

The last three days out, Mush made me navigator, a customary move designed to give the third officer experience. I had plenty of it. Right away we ran into a storm that lasted all the way to Pearl. On top of that, our high speed was drinking up the fuel at a terrific rate, and Mush refused to slow down to conserve fuel. Between wondering as navigator where in hell we were, and worrying as engineer whether we were going to make it without running out of fuel, I was too busy to enjoy the trip. We had to be escorted into Pearl — since the attack that had launched the war, orders had been to fire first at any unescorted submarine and ask questions later — and some of the longest hours of my life were spent off Oahu, waiting for that rendezvous. Until our escort came into sight, I could not rid myself of the nagging fear that I had slipped up somewhere in my navigating and might be several hundred miles from where I thought I was.

We made quite a stir when we slid into the dock at Pearl early in February with a broom flying at the masthead to show we had swept the seas clean — and with no more than two hundred gallons of fuel left in our tanks. The war correspondents had a field day. There were long accounts of the *Wahoo*'s third patrol and stories about her colorful skipper. Mush appeared on the *March of Time.* Back in Los Angeles, the day the story broke, the *Times* sent a reporter out to interview Mush's wife, who was living there with their two children. The big news was a surprise to her. Mush had talked to her by phone the day before, but all he had told her was that the *Wahoo* had done better than he had expected.

The rest of us spent a couple of days basking in his reflected glory, and then settled down to enjoy our leave at the Royal Hawaiian. Only one question troubled us. The word had spread that we were going to lose one of our officers. New submarines were coming off the ways at a rapid rate back in the States, new subs that required crews and experienced officers. The prospect that our beautifully coordinated team might be broken up was one we discussed with mixed feelings, for while none of us wanted to see another member of the team leave, any of us would have been willing to give up even the *Wahoo* in exchange for a few months back in the States while we commissioned and shook down a new boat.

I seemed to be the most likely candidate for a transfer. My seniority made me eligible for the second spot on a new sub, while Dick O'Kane was not quite to the point where he could expect a command of his own, and obviously he would not be taken off the *Wahoo* for anything less. I wrote to Ann that there was a pretty good chance I would be seeing her soon.

Then the blow fell. On the third day of our rest period, Mush came into my room one morning as I lay abed at the Royal. There was an ominously sympathetic look on his face as he handed me my orders: "When relieved from duties aboard the U.S.S. *Wahoo*, proceed and report to the commanding officer of the U.S.S. *Pollack* as executive officer."

I groaned. Even in the prewar days at Pearl when I had been aboard the *Skipjack*, the *Pollack* had been considered something less than the latest-type sub in the fleet. Built in the 1930s, she certainly would be a comedown from the *Wahoo*. And worst of all, she was right there in Pearl!

In short, instead of going home to new construction, I would take the place of another officer going home to new construction. Instead of a new boat, I would be on an old one. It was a promotion, but it wasn't worth it.

Mush grinned. "Hell, George, with you aboard she'll burn up the Pacific."

"Yes, but who's going to keep you and Dick out of trouble?"

He undertook to cheer me up by applying the same half nelson that had permanently bent my neck on the second patrol. "Don't worry," he grunted as we wrestled. "Roger is almost as big a sissy as you are. He'll take care of us."

Neither of us dreamed then that his words held a note of tragic prophecy, for there would come a time when Roger too left the *Wahoo*.

It was my close friend and classmate, Gus Weinel, who had been ordered back to new construction from the *Pollack* and whose place as executive officer I was to take. I drove back to Pearl the next day to congratulate him and take a look at my new home. There was one bright spot in the picture: my skipper would be Roby Palmer, an old friend from prewar days who had been partly responsible for my decision to transfer to submarines. He had been present when Ann and I were married the second, or official, time at Pearl in 1938. If I couldn't see Ann, at least I would be able to talk about her during the next patrol to someone who knew her.

It was almost a pleasure to see the look of joy on Gus Weinel's face when I found him in the forward battery. He had made about four runs on the *Pollack* and was certainly more deserving of a trip home than I. He wasted no time in idle talk.

"Welcome aboard! When can you relieve me?"

"Well," I said, "we can inventory equipment tomorrow, inventory confidential publications the day after, and confer on the third day. Maybe in about four days — " I had to stop before he hit me. Peacetime routine was one thing, and a wartime leave was another. So he shoved some papers under my nose and I signed. One declared that he and I had inventoried about twenty thousand dollars' worth of equipment, that it was all accounted for, and that henceforth I was responsible for it. Another certified that Gus and I and the communications officer, whom I hadn't even met, had inventoried the confidential publications. A third, dated a few days ahead, was a report to the captain, stating that I had officially relieved Gus as executive officer of the *Pollack*. Within minutes of the time we greeted one another, Gus was shaking hands with the *Pollack* officers and men and heading for the gangplank. Under his arm he carried the boxed sextant he had won at the Naval Academy for standing first in navigation.

I never saw him again. His new sub, the *Cisco*, which I so deeply envied him, was lost on her first patrol.

I was not officially attached to the *Pollack* until the date on the report to Captain Palmer. Meanwhile, it was time to relax. I wrote the sad news to Ann and settled down for a little fun. The war had worked tremendous changes in the social customs of Honolulu. Streets had to be cleared by ten o'clock at night; if you stayed beyond that hour, you simply spent the night where you were. And the general blackout had put a crimp in the large-scale parties for which prewar Honolulu had been famous. One night I went to Waikiki for a party given by a couple noted in the old days for lavish, heavy-drinking affairs that lasted all night. This one was a world removed. We had charcoal-broiled steaks out in the back yard before dark, and then sat around in the moonlight and talked. The party was over by nine.

But one thing that hadn't changed was spear fishing. I had developed a love for it in the days when I was stationed in Pearl on the *Skipjack,* though back in those days it was called goggle fishing. Chester Nimitz, Jr., my classmate and opposite number on the *Sturgeon,* and I had bought crude Japanese equipment and learned the sport. Now, the first Sunday after the *Wahoo* returned to port, I persuaded Roger Paine to go with me for a try at spearing a few fish. We borrowed the jeep from the submarine tender and drove out to a rocky shore at Waianae on the west coast of the island.

We actually speared some fish, and in that peaceful setting, out of sight and feel of the war, I had one of the big scares of my life. We were both about fifty yards from shore, lazily diving and surfacing in the crystal water, when I looked over my shoulder and saw a mammoth shark. He was absolutely motionless, looking at me with as cold a stare as I ever expect to see. Roger hadn't seen him.

I remembered having read in Dr. Victor Heiser's autobiography how he had once escaped from sharks by moving away very, very slowly. Just what the philosophy was behind the plan I didn't remember, but I grasped desperately at the technique. Carefully and ever so casually I began to inch toward the shore, afraid to yell "Shark!" lest Roger churn the water white and get us both killed. I had no reason to expect that he had read the same book.

After a lifetime of agony, I got safely out of range, increased my pace, and clambered up on the rocks at last. Roger was still in the shark's area. I called to him with great nonchalance, "Say, Roger, can you come over here a minute?" But something in my voice gave me away. Roger came roaring in like a speedboat — no shark in the world could have overtaken him — and leaped out of the water, his face pale as a sheet. He was considerably aroused when I explained my carefully thought-out plan of action, and insisted that the real truth of the matter was that I had left him out there as a decoy. He even blamed me when it developed he had plowed his furrow through the water so frantically that his class ring had slipped off his finger. We discussed the advisability of giving the shark a decent time to depart and going back in search of the ring, but by then neither of us was willing to trust the other, let alone the shark.

We got back to the tender about eight that night to find the commander roaring mad because his jeep had been gone all day. He had forgotten he had lent it to us. When we reminded him, he seemed so mollified that we borrowed it again to go back to the Royal Hawaiian for the night, promising to have it back the first thing in the morning. But one thing led to another that night, and we didn't get back to the tender until about ten the next morning. It was a lucky thing for us, as I wrote to Ann, that for the moment the men of the *Wahoo* could do no wrong.

I thought ruefully of this glory by association, now denied to me, when I went back to the *Wahoo* the next day to take a final look around and collect my gear. Among the prizes I brought away was one that every man on the boat envied me: the homemade chart of Wewak harbor, created with such frantic zeal during the early days of the third patrol. A big controversy over who should keep the chart had arisen a few days before we returned to Pearl, and Mush, who never pulled his rank in such matters, had suggested that we deal a cold deck with the chart as a prize. I drew a flush.

I was to see Mush Morton once more, when the *Pollack* put into Midway the following April and tied up across the dock from the *Wahoo*.

We had run into foul weather that delayed our arrival, and my old shipmates on the *Wahoo*, knowing I was navigator, had read the dispatch announcing the delay with great glee. As we pulled alongside, Mush and Dick were standing on the dock, looking up at me.

"What happened, George?" Mush called innocently. "Forget about the International Date Line?"

"Aw, Captain," Dick explained, loud enough for every man aboard the *Pollack* to hear, "he just got lost again."

The *Wahoo* had just arrived from a furious patrol in the Yellow Sea during which it had sunk nine enemy ships. Mush's eyes were still alight from his fresh conquests of the enemy, and Dick was more his new self than ever, sure, steady, and confident. And the officers of the *Wahoo* had a story to tell that was to become a classic wherever subs tied up in the Pacific during the remainder of the war. I heard it at the club that evening.

On their last patrol, they had taken another makey-learn, a very senior commander, senior even to Mush himself, and he had rapidly developed grave reservations about the manner in which the *Wahoo* conducted a war patrol. He had taken exception to what he called a lack of planning, poor coordination, and an absence of discipline in the conning tower during attacks. All this, in spite of the tremendous record Mush had made on the patrol, he had reported to the squadron commander the moment the *Wahoo* arrived at Midway.

He was being transferred off the *Wahoo* anyhow, but when Dick and the others learned of the report, they decided to hasten his departure. Dick himself, or so the story went, stalked down to the boat and had the commander's effects gathered up and set on the dock, and when the departing makey-learn arrived to pack, he discovered orders had been left that he was not to be allowed aboard. Whether these were the exact facts or not I do not know to this day, but at any rate the critic was gone by now, and the officers of the *Wahoo* told one hilarious story after another at the bar that night about their experiences with him on the patrol.

The change Mush had wrought in these men was marvelous. No abler, happier, and more competent men ever operated a submarine. To an outsider, the *Wahoo* may well have appeared a little loose in the conning tower, but the proof of command is in results, and the results were there for all to see. Furthermore, if the makey-learn had observed any lack of decision during the patrol, he must have been vastly impressed with the swift and decisive action taken at Midway when the honor of the conning tower was sullied.

It had been a tremendous patrol, topping the war's record to that date in the number of ships sunk. Mush had gone into the sea lanes between China and Korea, again returning only after every torpedo had been expended. Even as we came into Midway, I had seen the familiar broom lashed to his periscope.

As events were to turn out, the *Wahoo* had just completed her most successful patrol. She would go on to become a legend, but a tragic one. Before the end of the year, a combination of circumstances would arise which, by the very nature of her skipper's magnificent courage, would send her to her doom with all the inexorability of a Greek tragedy.

After I saw her that last time at Midway, the *Wahoo* went on another patrol, sank three ships, and was ordered back to Mare Island Navy Yard for an overhaul. While she was there, Dick O'Kane was given his own command, the new submarine *Tang*. It was a great loss for Mush, of course, but Roger Paine was there to move up into the executive officer's position, and the *Wahoo* might have gone on to even greater exploits had not two more blows fallen.

The night before she left Pearl on her first patrol after the overhaul, Roger had an attack of appendicitis. They hauled him off to the hospital and put in his place a capable officer, but one who knew Mush by his awesome reputation rather than by long association. It was a difference, I have always felt, that was to prove fatal. For by now virtually all Mush's old associates in the conning tower were gone, replaced by men who naturally thought of their great and famous skipper as infallible. I believe that, on previous patrols, Mush had come to rely subconsciously on his officers to tell him what not to do, and with the loss of Roger this safety factor disappeared. Here was a man whose valor blazed up so brightly that at times he could not distinguish between the calculated risk and the foolhardy chance, and now the men who knew him well enough to insist on pointing out the difference were gone.

The patrol that followed, the *Wahoo*'s sixth, would have driven even a less volatile man than Mush Morton to furious incaution. For this time, in company with the *Plunger*, the *Wahoo* ventured into the Sea of Japan itself — and to no avail. After making the hazardous run past the Kuriles and through the narrow La Pérouse Strait into what was virtually the Emperor's wading pool, Mush hunted down and attacked nine Japanese vessels in four days without scoring a hit. The whole desperate gamble had failed because the *Wahoo* had a load of malfunctioning torpedoes.

Ten times Mush gave the order to fire, and each time the torpedoes, whose very wakes in those heavily guarded waters could cost the life of every man aboard, failed miserably. They broached, or made erratic runs, or even banged into the hulls of the targets like lifeless hunks of scrap iron. After the tenth was fired, Mush sent off a bitter message to ComSubPac, which promptly recalled him to Pearl with the remaining useless torpedoes aboard.

Even this time, Mush did not return without trophies. The *Wahoo* sank four sampans on its return trip out of the Sea of Japan, and brought along six Japanese fishermen for questioning. But it was a grim skipper who came into Pearl to get rid of his faulty munitions, and he coupled with his report the insistent request that he be allowed to return immediately to the same patrol area with a new cargo of torpedoes.

So it was that the *Wahoo* left on its seventh patrol for waters so perilous they were shortly to be abandoned as a patrol area, and with a skipper so enraged he was ready to take any chance to redeem his boat's proud record, and with a fire-control party that did not know him well enough to try to hold him in check.

They stopped briefly at Midway for fuel. It was the last time the *Wahoo* or any of her crew was ever seen. What happened before she went down remains a mystery to this day. A study of Japanese records after the war indicated Mush probably sank four Japanese ships on that last patrol. But somewhere in the process, perhaps at La Pérouse Strait, where the Japanese attacked an unidentified submarine in October, 1943, the *Wahoo* herself was lost. She was a mighty warrior, skippered by the most valiant man I ever knew.

Dick O'Kane left the *Wahoo* to write his own brilliant chapter in the records of submarine warfare. The man who had been the perfect executive officer for Mush Morton became the perfect skipper of the *Tang*.

The *Tang* was in action less than a year, but in that time it also became a legend in the Pacific. It sank more enemy ships than any other submarine except the *Tautog*, and ranked fourth in tonnage sunk. On its third patrol alone, the *Tang* took a toll of ten ships totaling more than thirty-nine thousand tons — more ships sunk during a single war patrol than by any other United States submarine, a distinction Dick thus took away from his old skipper. In April, 1944, he set another record that was to stand for more than a year, rescuing no fewer than twenty-two airmen in a lifeguard operation during a carrier strike at Truk. Six months later, in the middle of a war patrol in the East China Sea that had already netted seven enemy ships, O'Kane and the *Tang* became involved in a tragedy submariners will talk about for generations — the case of the submarine that sank itself.

A torpedo fired at a transport already crippled by the *Tang*'s marksmen suddenly swerved to the left, made a hairpin turn, and returned to blast the submarine in the stern only twenty seconds after it was fired. Dick and eight others on the bridge at the time were thrown overboard, and the submarine sank in 180 feet of water. The trapped men fought their way to the forward compartment and had gathered at the escape hatch when a Japanese warship overhead hit them with a depth charge. Even so, thirteen crew members eventually escaped from the forward compartment. Eight reached the surface alive, and five were able to swim until morning. They were picked up, along with Dick and three other survivors of the bridge, by a Japanese destroyer escort, and spent the remainder of the war in Japanese prison camps. Dick O'Kane returned home after the war to receive the Congressional Medal of Honor. His great submarine, which in only about nine months of action had sunk twenty-four vessels totaling more than ninety thousand tons of enemy shipping, was one of but two submarines to receive the Presidential Unit Citation twice for its work.

8

The Old Lady

I LEFT the *Wahoo* with great sadness. Under the rigorous training of Marvin Kennedy and the glorious leadership of Mush Morton she had blossomed into a tremendous fighting machine. Her morale was at an absolute peak, and anyone who left her in those days for whatever reason did so with some reluctance. A fighting craft becomes more than a place to live and work for the men who serve on her. She has a personality of her own, and especially in wartime her men develop attitudes toward her which are grounded far more deeply in emotion than in logic. To those of us who had made three patrols on her the *Wahoo* had become part warrior comrade, part glorious Amazon, and part bawd — a burly, confident, reckless wench with a touch of coarseness and an overwhelming and often exhausting claim on our emotions.

The *Pollack* was different. She was much older, for one thing, and more delicate. She had ailments that should have disqualified her for war service long since, but she was neither frowzy nor bitter. There was about her a deceptive air of leisurely gentility — deceptive only in that, when action was called for, she was always ready to try a little more than her frail constitution could stand. And she was eccentric, in a sly, almost gentle way that made you sense there was far more depth to her character than to that of most brash young submarines. Coming to her weary from the strain of three war patrols and disappointed at not getting a leave home to new construction, I soon found her one of the most memorable old ladies I was ever to know.

She had been on her way to Pearl from San Francisco when the war began. A week after the Japanese attack, she was on her way, under command of Lieutenant Commander S. P. Moseley, to the area of Tokyo Bay — one of the first three American submarines to go out on a war patrol from Pearl Harbor. The first Japanese merchantman to be sunk by the Pacific Fleet Submarine Force was sunk by the *Pollack*.

And, as befitted a pioneer, she had special and quite remarkable arrangements ashore for her officers. I learned of them after my first day aboard. When four o'clock came, I noticed a general stir of preparation among the officers who were going off duty.

"Come on, George," Roby Palmer said, "let's go out to the Hale Wahine."

"What's that?" I asked, knowing full well that *hale wahine* means "house of girls."

Roby just grinned at me. "You'll see," he promised, and we all piled into the jeep assigned to the *Pollack* and drove out into Manoa Valley, on Armstrong Street, until we came to a big two-story house with a comfortable, homey look.

"This is it," Roby said. The other officers piled out, but Roby put a hand on my knee. "Maybe I'd better explain first," he said. And so I got my introduction to one of the most unusual and wonderful institutions of the war.

The Hale Wahine was a household of six or seven American girls who had survived the shipment back to the mainland of most of the civilian personnel in Honolulu. Most of them worked for the Navy or the Army. They were all girls of fine families, and their families had friends in Honolulu who kept a careful eye on them. They were living together for convenience, sharing a maid and taking turns as housekeepers. Early in the war, some far-seeing officer of the *Pollack* had carefully and decorously cultivated the friendship of these young ladies, with such happy results that their house was open to the officers of the *Pollack* whenever they were in port.

It was a relationship that depended on a rigid code of propriety. Everyone realized one step over the line would somehow put a curse on the whole arrangement, and no officer of the *Pollack* would have dared incur the wrath of his fellows by doing anything that would cut them off from this oasis of beauty and decency in a desert of war.

Roby explained all this to me, and then took me in and introduced me to Trudie Kraft and Sorrel Wainwright and the others as the new executive officer of the *Pollack*. We had dinner there and sat around for an hour or two, talking, playing cards, and planning a picnic. By the time we left I felt I had known them all my life.

It was about three weeks before the *Pollack* was ready for sea again, and during that time the Hale Wahine became as nearly a part of home to me as anything could be without Ann and Billy. It is hard to explain how refreshing and restful "polite society" can be to someone accustomed for months on end to the companionship of no one but other hairy, bad-smelling men. We had picnics and dances, and dinners at the Hale, and dinners at the Royal Hawaiian. Everything the girls could do to make life pleasant for a bunch of lonesome sailors they did, always within the bounds of propriety. Curfew was at nine, and we were generally gone by then, though occasionally we found ourselves wandering back to the Royal Hawaiian after hours, very fearful of being picked up and wondering whether any MP in the world would believe the innocent nature of our evening's activities. The second floor of the Hale Wahine was the dormitory part, and thus off limits to us, but we had the run of the ground floor — the kitchen, the dining room, the big living room. We officers did a great deal of cooking. That was where I first discovered my great talent as a chef, a talent that consisted principally of putting every condiment on the shelves into anything I cooked.

During the whole three weeks before the *Pollack* was ready for action, I never got over a sense of unbelief at our good fortune. I was as amazed as if I had said "Open sesame" and a cave filled with jewels had opened before me.

As executive officer of the *Pollack* I was to be her navigator, and the prospect worried me. Gus Weinel, whose place I was taking, was a man whose skill at navigating was known by every member of our class at the Naval Academy, while my own navigating was more than a little rusty, as my experience in bringing the *Wahoo* home had reminded me.

But for all her frailty, the *Pollack* proved to be a comfortable boat to navigate, and when we departed Pearl early in March, 1943, after a three-day training period, I was already looking forward to the patrol as a sort of vacation. Captain Roby Palmer and I were old and close friends, and I knew him as an amiable man and a fine commanding officer. Our orders called for us to proceed first to Makin Island, an atoll on the north end of the Gilberts — an area which at that time was not exceptionally hot. I hoped the end of the patrol would bring me orders home. And the crew, officers and men alike, were mostly veterans of the *Pollack* since even before the war had begun, and long seasoning had given them a relaxed attitude toward everything she did. At her age and with her infirmities, she was not going to burn up the seas. When a crisis arose, she would give all she had and a little more, but meanwhile life would go on, so why not make it as pleasant as possible?

And life was pleasant on the *Pollack*. She boasted refinements of entertainment that other submarines lacked. The men of the *Pollack*, for example, played chess. Every man aboard played chess, and most of them played it very well indeed and with no consideration for rank or seniority. On their last patrol, they had conducted a tournament which reached its climax when the brilliant Gus Weinel opposed a Negro steward's mate in the finals. Gus had lost.

I had played chess occasionally before, but compared with most of these men I was the rankest beginner. And too, they had taken some strange and wonderful liberties with the rulebook which I had to learn in order to hold my own. In the *Pollack* version of chess, the idea was not only to outwit your opponent, but to overpower him as well. If you realized after making a move that it was the wrong one, and if you could take it back before your opponent stopped you, it was all right. It took me quite a while to grow accustomed to the sight of a player leaping across the wardroom table, grabbing his opponent's arms, and holding them down while he made his own move with his teeth.

So we set out in about as carefree a mood as is possible on a submarine bound for enemy waters, and I began my indoctrination into the mystic order of navigation. There was plenty of time for it, for only two distractions occurred during the first week and a half of the patrol. One was an acute attack of appendicitis suffered by one of our seamen, a man named Hamilton, who was treated with cold packs and sulfathiazole and made the entire patrol in reasonable comfort despite the impassioned pleas of our pharmacist's mate for permission to undertake a do-it-yourself appendectomy. The other was an aerial attack our sixth day out. We went down to a hundred and fifty feet before the bomb fell, and the *Pollack* hardly shivered. At the time, I was so concerned over my first landfall that I barely noticed it.

It will be obvious that navigation is, if anything, even more important to a submarine than to other ships. And there were fewer gimmicks then than now for making it easy. You had to know celestial navigation, and know it well enough to keep your doubts in the background, or you were out of luck. Oftentimes, you had to take your star sights after dark — a technique originated by submarines,

I believe. This involved bringing the star's image down
to a horizon which you could only guess at, but which had
to be guessed with considerable accuracy. As we neared
Tarawa, which we were supposed to raise on March 16, I
began trying some of the techniques I had heard other navi-
gators talk about. The problem of taking star sights after
dark, for example, was easier if you cut a pair of binoculars
in two and used one half as a telescope in the sextant in
order to see the horizon.

By the morning of the sixteenth, I felt reasonably sure
Tarawa would show up on schedule. But it didn't. We proceeded submerged all day in what I was sure was the direction of the island without sighting it. The jokesters in the
conning tower rode me unmercifully. But when we surfaced that night and got a good fix, I was able to produce
an alibi. The current had reversed itself from the day before.
We raised Makin on schedule, just before dawn, and I was
excused for missing the landfall the previous day. We patrolled off Makin for a day, saw nothing but some enemy
planes, and proceeded according to orders to Jaluit, the
largest of the nearby Marshall Islands.

The vacation came to an abrupt end two days later. In
midafternoon, while we were patrolling on a line between
Jaluit and Makin, smoke was sighted thirteen miles away
to the southeast. As we drew closer, we found it was a
freighter with two patrol vessels off her bows. We fired
four torpedoes and thought we heard one hit, but there was
no time to find out then for sure; the two escorts drove us
under and gave us a terrific depth-charge attack.

About two hours later we surfaced to resume the chase.

It was around eight o'clock, and the moon shone down on that tropical water almost as brilliantly as it does in the movies. In fact, it was too bright for our purposes, for it made a surface attack too dangerous. On the other hand, it wasn't quite bright enough for a periscope attack, so we had to track the target all night, keeping ahead of it and planning to submerge at dawn for the kill. I found myself completely unable to sleep that night. This was my first experience as executive officer during an attack, and the target was in plain sight astern. Instead of resting quietly until morning, I went up on the bridge every half hour or so to take a look.

As is usual in those latitudes, the sky clouded up about half an hour before sunrise and rain squalls filled the area. We turned toward the target, dived, and came up to periscope depth in the middle of a rain squall. Roby took the periscope while I stood beside him, operating the is-was and translating his sightings. We got in to eight hundred yards and fired three torpedoes. Two of them exploded, but before we could look for the damage, we had to go deep, for Roby spotted one of the escorts only three hundred yards away and headed at us.

On our way down, three of the poppet valves stuck open in the forward torpedo room, and before the emergency valves on the torpedo tubes could be closed, there were six inches of water over the deck plates. But after thus demonstrating that she was as unpredictable as ever, the *Pollack* then stood up to one of the most severe depth-charge attacks she had ever experienced, and with no apparent damage other than the usual peeling of paint and pushing in of cables. We finally pumped the bilges, reloaded, and came back to periscope depth three hours after our attack. There was no sign of the ship. In the absence of positive evidence, we didn't get official credit for sinking it, but I believe we did.

Moments of crisis become blurred in memory while insignificant events often remain crystal clear for a lifetime. I suppose this is because, although the conscious mind sets the crises apart as things to remember, the unconscious undertakes to wipe out the elements of fear and insecurity, so that finally you do not really remember the event itself, but only the fact that it happened. Not so with the minor, humorous events, the happenings in which tension is absent. These often remain as clear and immediate in memory as if they had occurred yesterday. Such a thing happened to me that day as the *Pollack* groped back toward the surface from deep submergence after the danger had ended.

We were all haggard from the all-night chase, the attack, and the depth-charging. After the escorts stopped dropping charges and went away, almost everyone not on watch turned in. As the propeller noises faded, Roby turned to me and said, "Bring her up to periscope depth, George. I'm going to turn in. Man, I'm tired."

He looked it, too: tired and a little wild. He dropped down the hatch, leaving only me and our reliable quartermaster, Few, in the conning tower. I observed that Few, too, looked haggard and drawn. I had been up longer than anyone, but it did not occur to me until later that I must have looked even wilder than both of them.

As the boat neared periscope depth, I raised the scope, put my eye to it, and began to look at the dimly lighted water while the tip of the periscope was still about ten feet under. It is a rare thing to see marine life through a periscope, perhaps because the bulk of the submarine scares fish away, but on this morning as I gazed through the water I saw a real monster.

He was green. He had a huge head, out of all proportion to his body. He trailed long, filamentlike whiskers as he swam lazily toward the periscope, and his large, sinister eyes stared straight into mine.

"Damn!" I whispered. "Few, come look at this thing! There's a sea monster out there!"

With some hesitation, Few moved over for a look. I almost forced his eye to the scope in my eagerness to share this unusual sight.

"Look at those eyes!" I urged. "Did you ever see anything with whiskers like that? And the color! Isn't that the damnedest green you ever saw?"

Few grunted a polite and thoroughly unrewarding agreement and stood back. A few seconds later the periscope tip broke water and we began our day's routine. After a sweep around the horizon, I lowered the periscope and leaned against the side of the conning tower wearily to talk to Few. He was not usually reticent, but by now he had withdrawn to the farthest corner of the conning tower, and my attempts at conversation failed. I gave it up, and for a while we stood in silence.

"Mr. Grider," Few said at last with elaborate unconcern, "do you feel all right?"

Then it dawned on me. "Few," I said, "didn't you see that fish?"

"No, sir."

To this day, Few probably thinks there wasn't one. But there was. . . . I think.

For more than three weeks we patrolled off the Marshalls and Jaluit with only one incident, an attack on a steamer headed into Jaluit. We fired two torpedoes and heard a couple of explosions, but again an attack sent us under without an opportunity to confirm the sinking.

Maneuvers that were simple on other submarines were often complicated on the *Pollack,* and this particular submerging was no exception. For whereas you can normally hope to evade a destroyer by going deep and running silent, we couldn't shake this one. The *Pollack,* which leaked air and oil constantly when we were submerged, was no doubt leaving an oil slick above us for the destroyer to follow.

The depth charges continued, uncomfortably close, for hours. We had been submerged all day and half the night and our battery, which was never strong, was getting very weak.

About midnight, Roby decided we would have to surface and take our chances with the destroyer.

It was an unusually tense moment. Roby was at the periscope in the conning tower, which we had made as dark as possible in the vain hope that by adapting his eyes the skipper could see something through the scope. Orders were whispered down the hatch to the lookouts to come up from the control room, so that when we surfaced they would be able to rush up onto the bridge and start looking for the destroyer.

And now, as if the *Pollack* had grown weary of the mounting tension, it was raucously broken.

Both lookouts were wearing dark-adaption glasses, which made the conning tower they were climbing into even darker. The first up the ladder, an Italian boy noted as a great joker, thought the other was ahead of him. As he came up the hatch into the tiny conning tower where the captain squatted before the partly-raised periscope, his head bumped soundly against Roby's rear. Thinking he had collided with his fellow lookout, he reached for the darkened fanny above him and gave it a strong pinch.

"Who," he squeaked in a high falsetto, "is dis?"

Roby was a man who could rise to all occasions.

"Dis," he squeaked back, "is de captain." Then, raising his voice to a roar, "WHO IS DAT?"

We surfaced a minute or two later, the destroyer failed to spot us, and we got safely out of the area. I have always believed that, without that slapstick exchange to ease the pressure, it might have ended otherwise.

That was all the combat excitement we had for the remainder of the patrol, but we had plenty of another kind before we reached Midway. The *Pollack*'s newspaper sponsored an election.

Our mimeographed newspaper was another distinction of the *Pollack*. It came out every day, full of news, gossip, and scandal about everybody aboard. It carried news about the war, picked up by our radioman, but this was only incidental. Everyone contributed poetry, jokes, and fantastic stories to it, and one of the sailors blessed with a talent for caricature drew regular cartoons for it. All of us had been lampooned by him at one time or another, Jack Jackson the most recently.

Jack was the commissary officer, a young naval reserve from California who was new at submarining and who, when he was given his turns at taking the *Pollack* under, was constantly having trouble keeping her on an even keel. The stern had broached so often during his dives that one day the newspaper came out with a cartoon entitled "Mr. Jackson's Dive." It showed the stern completely out of water, propeller churning, while sailors sat and lay about the deck fishing, sleeping, or taking exercises. A man at the open hatch was shouting, "The Captain says you guys have to come below now. We're going to try and get the stern under again."

Now, as monotony settled over us all, someone on the newspaper came up with an idea: we could elect a Sweetheart of the *Pollack*. As executive officer I had to pass on the plan, and it struck me as an unusually good morale builder. For days, nothing at all had happened. We would remain submerged until dark, seeing nothing, then surface, patrol slowly until dawn while we charged the batteries, and submerge again. We needed some kind of excitement. So we appointed two nominating committees, and they picked two candidates for the great honor about to be bestowed, and the campaign got under way.

The plan, which, as I recall, was never carried out, was to send the winner a notification and a hula skirt when we got back to Pearl. But this aspect of it was secondary; the main thing was simply the idea of holding an election. The two candidates chosen were Betty Hutton and Anne Sheridan, and electioneering was allowed to continue for four or five days. We turned over the internal-communications system to the two hastily formed political parties, and speeches sounded throughout the compartments of the *Pollack* every night. On the night before the election there was actually a torchlight parade: the men marched through the narrow passageways waving torches made from rags soaked in diesel oil, shouting wildly for Betty or Anne.

It had become obvious early in the campaign that the election would have to be supervised with utmost care, because charges were bruited about that certain leaders on both sides were not above the use of tricks and chicanery. So it was decided to place the ballot box on the table directly in front of the diving officer. There is always a diving officer in the control room when the boat is submerged, and on this patrol the diving officer had had nothing exciting to do for days, so we knew there would be no minute of the day in which the ballot box, lying within six inches of his nose, would be out of his sight. Of course, if a Japanese target did come along, the election would be canceled.

It was further decided, as a safeguard to the democratic processes, that voters would approach in single file and each would personally hand his marked ballot to the diving officer. The officer would check it to be sure there was only one piece of paper before he dropped it into the box.

Election day came, and voting proceeded in good order, without violence and exactly according to the rules. By six o'clock everyone had voted. Congratulating ourselves on the trim efficiency with which the operation had been carried out, we sat down to count the ballots. The final tally showed Miss Sheridan the victor by a vote of 275 to 194.

At that time there were about ninety officers and enlisted men on the *Pollack*.

The election officials destroyed the ballots, declared it no contest, and repeated the election the next day. This time considerable improvement was noted — the total vote was only 262 — but being perfectionists, we threw that one out too and called for a final, airtight, official election.

At this point, with fiendishly cunning timing, the adherents of Miss Hutton launched a whispering campaign against her adversary. Suddenly the report raced the length of the *Pollack* that Miss Sheridan wore padding. Within hours it was being repeated openly and without contradiction. Miss Hutton won the election (the final vote was 103 to 70) and to this day I do not know whether the claims of her adherents were true or false.

I was glad when the distractions of the election were behind us, for we were fast approaching Midway by now, and I wanted to spend as much time as possible practicing my navigation. Once, and I state it with considerable pride, I got a three-star fix at noon. That means I took the sun sight, the moon sight, and the sight of Venus in broad daylight, and got a fix right down to a pinpoint. Any navigator who reads this will appreciate what it means. Most people are not aware that you can see Venus in the daytime, but if you know where to look, and if Venus is not too close to the sun, you can see it on any clear day. When you have a new moon or a half-moon, you can shoot it in the daytime, too. And when you get all three — sun, moon, and Venus — you are entitled to brag. I tried to tell that to my old shipmates from the *Wahoo* when we moored alongside them at Midway about the middle of April, but they wouldn't listen. They were too delighted over the fact that I had brought the *Pollack* in a day late.

Despite my pleasure at seeing Mush, Dick, Roger, and the others from my old boat, the rest period at Midway was nothing to cheer about. Submariners accustomed to taking their ease at the Royal Hawaiian between patrols were never able to appreciate the limited luxuries of Midway. My memories of that interlude run largely to gooney birds.

Gooney birds are albatrosses, graceful beyond description in flight and ludicrous beyond belief on the ground. Midway was full of them. They stood about in groups of two or three, facing one another, and performed incredible rites. First they clashed beaks like two ungainly fencers with heavy swords. Then they stretched heads and beaks skyward in unison and uttered lugubrious sounds, full of sorrow and longing. Finally they made complete waddling turns, thrust their beaks under their uplifted wings, stood there for a moment, and then repeated the entire ceremony. It must have been a form of mating dance, but no one ever reported seeing them mate, and they were closely watched.

These unfortunate fowls were addicted to beer, which was offered to them in great quantities by bored military personnel, and which added considerably to the lurchiness of their dances. A refinement of this technique was developed during our stay by the *Pollack*'s gayest bachelor, Dick Zullinger, who was even more embittered than the rest of us to be resting and relaxing on Midway in the utter absence of any feminine companionship. Zully fed the gooney birds Manhattans. In all the world I have never seen but one sight more outlandish than a drunken gooney bird, and I saw that at Midway too. It was a pair of drunken submariners trying to imitate gooney birds.

There were also moaning birds on Midway. These, I believe, are known more exactly as wedge-tailed shearwaters, but their nickname fitted them to perfection. They had tunneled nests into the sand all over the island, and all night, every night, they would lie there in the sand and moan like despairing women. We could hear them from our rooms in the Gooney Bird Hotel, a little frame structure that had been put up before the war, and it was a desolate and disturbing sound.

There was plenty of time, after our visits to the officers' club or the movies, to think long thoughts of home, and I expect all of us filled our letters with more sentiment than usual. One of my letters to Ann (all of which she saved, as wives do, for some improbable time when she might want to go back and read them) demonstrates just how fervently poetic a seaman can get on a lonely atoll a whole world removed from the people he loves best.

I was explaining why I was sometimes quite late in answering specific comments or questions in her letters. "Maybe you won't understand this," I wrote, "but it's true, and the reason lies somewhere in the fact that I love you so deeply and frantically. I can't even read your letters when they're first handed to me. I thumb through them quickly to see which one is the freshest; I nervously tear that one open and read the last page to make certain that you and Billy are well; I then breathe a mighty sigh of relief, stuff them all in my pocket, and go about my business. In the still of the night, when all the problems of the day have been settled and I am alone, I very carefully break them out, and in the hush of my lonely bunk I tenderly and lovingly read them one by one, smiling here, laughing there, and sometimes blinking the tears of love and loneliness out of my eyes. After I have read them all and reread them, I lie there and think about you and Billy. . . ."

A steady diet of gooney birds can bring out talents in a man he never dreamed he had.

9

Frustration

CHANGES WERE IN THE WORKS for the *Pollack*. Roby Palmer was going home to New London to join the staff of the Submarine School, and Lieutenant Commander B. E. Lewellen would take his place. We were losing three officers as well. Zully would remain with us, a fine officer at sea for all his high jinks ashore, and I was glad of it. I was equally pleased over the departure of one of the officers. A submarine is a very small place to live in, and idiosyncrasies that are only mildly irritating in larger areas can become intolerable in a wardroom midway through a long patrol. This young lieutenant had a habit of pulling at his eyebrows. It was a small thing, but he made the most of it. Day after day, with infuriating detachment, he worried his brows until someone would shout a threat to hit him if he didn't stop it. Such a thing, like the nail in the shoe of the general's horse, can grow important enough to affect battles and alter or even terminate men's lives. I could only hope that his next shipmates were men whose nerves were calmer than ours.

We did the best we could to enjoy the remaining days of

our leave. We bowled and went deep-sea fishing, and when my commission as lieutenant commander came through, we threw a party that had the officers' club rocking. On the night Roby flew back to Pearl we had another. Envious of his luck but encouraged by this evidence we were not forgotten by the higher echelons, I broke a stern personal rule and wrote to Ann that I had excellent prospects of a leave when we came in from the next patrol. I had tried to avoid all such speculation in my letters, knowing how easy it is to build up false hopes, but the signs looked good and the temptation was too great. Perhaps I would be holding my wife and son in my arms by early summer!

After all the days of idleness, we had a minor crisis the morning we left. Bud Cooper, our third officer and one of the best men aboard, was one of the three scheduled for transfers. Twice the orders arrived, twice Bud got ready to leave in a happy trance, and twice they were canceled. He was desperately anxious for the orders, but our new skipper was just as hopeful, for his own reasons, that they wouldn't come. Lewellen didn't at all like the idea of taking the *Pollack* out for the first time without its capable engineering officer. On the morning of May 10, after our engines had already been started, Bud's orders arrived. The skipper tried to persuade him it was too late for him to leave, but Bud said he thought he could make it. He went below, got all his gear together, and was ashore exactly ten minutes after the orders arrived. So we set off for the Marshalls with a new skipper and three new officers.

A week and a half later I was given the opportunity to make my first wartime attack. We had sunk a small

freighter the day before, off the coast of Wotje, after playing cat-and-mouse with it for three days before it came far
enough out of a lagoon for us to attack. The next day, off
Jaluit, we sighted a seven-thousand-ton freighter escorted
by a torpedo boat, and Captain Lew told me to take over.
It was a totally unexpected favor, and a major one. I had
told him, of course, about the *Wahoo* procedure, in which
the exec did all the periscope work, but it takes an iron will
for the man in command to turn over his only source of information about the enemy to a junior. I was childishly
grateful to Lewellen for doing it — and I gave him good
reason to wish he hadn't.

The approach was routine, but not for me. Here I was,
taking all the looks and issuing all the orders as we moved in
for the kill. In my enthusiasm, I concentrated on the
freighter and nothing else.

Finally we were in attack position and all was ready.

"We're all set, Captain. Shall I shoot?"

"Whenever you're ready, George. Where's the escort?"

"Stand by One. FIRE One!"

"Where's the escort, George?"

"Stand by Two. . . . FIRE Two. . . . FIRE Three.
. . . FIRE Four!"

"George. Take a sweep around for the escort."

"They're running straight, Captain. Headed right at
him . . . getting closer . . . wow!"

The first hit was followed by a second, and a third, and
then the fourth torpedo blasted the freighter's tail clean out
of the water. I was shouting almost hysterically when the
captain's roar silenced me.

"George, *where the hell is the damned escort?*"

It was the first time his question had penetrated. I swept the scope around, reported absently that the escort was coming in fast, bearing about thirty relative, angle on the bow zero. Then, still intoxicated by my magnificent attack, I looked back at the freighter.

"He's breaking up, Captain. He's sinking. He — hey, bring me up!"

The periscope had dipped under water. Lewellen had finally taken over.

We took a terrible depth-charging, complicated by a typical *Pollack* mishap. The bow planes jammed on hard dive, a leak was reported in the after battery, and the main motor contactors jumped out. Then, just while we were trying desperately to run silent, the auxiliary contactors jumped in and all the pumps in the engine room started running. That was one thing about the *Pollack:* you got to the point where you worried more over what she would do to herself than what the enemy would do to her. But, and this seemed to be another property of the *Pollack*, she survived all the difficulties and got us safely away at last.

We stayed out a month longer without sinking any more enemy ships, though we did have two memorable experiences. The first came on a quiet Sunday when we were running submerged and the sea above was full of rain squalls. A cribbage game was going on in the wardroom. I had never felt safer, more relaxed, more utterly convinced that we were far removed from any conceivable hazard.

Suddenly we were shaken by two colossal explosions, so unexpected that they dazed us. I was halfway to the control room before my feet hit the floor.

The depth bombs, dropped by some flier who must have

had the keenest nose for submarines in all the Japanese armed forces, had almost finished us. They came close to smashing the conning tower. They did flatten our searchlight and break the thick glass in the gyro repeater on the bridge. The overwhelming suddenness of that surprise attack on a serene Sunday was, for me, one of the biggest shocks of the war.

It worked wonders for our general sense of alertness, and a few days later when we sighted what looked like a fairly large sailing vessel east of Jaluit we took no chances. We decided to make a battle surface on it and came charging up out of the water as if it were the biggest prize in the Pacific. We had opened fire with our three-inch deck gun before we realized that it was much closer and considerably smaller than it had looked through the periscope. It was little more than a rowboat, in fact. We ceased fire, closed in on it, and found five frightened natives aboard. In an expansive mood, we handed them some cigarettes and bread and let them go.

It served to demonstrate, in the days ahead, how dangerous a virtue kindness can be in wartime. For Japanese planes gave us fits day and night for the next week. That little sailboat had hurried into Jaluit with our cigarettes and bread and reported our position to the enemy.

Bad news awaited us at Pearl. While the *Pollack* was away on its two patrols, every last girl at the Hale Wahine had got herself engaged. And this time there would be no replacements to keep the household going. They were all moving out and the house would be sold.

We knew the men the girls were engaged to. Most of them had desk jobs at Pearl, and they were a nice bunch of fellows, but the thought of them moving brazenly in and destroying our comfortable arrangement outraged us. We talked it over and hit upon a plan to break the engagements.

It was not merely a bad plan, it was probably the worst plan ever devised, and it was doomed to failure from the start. But in our state of righteous wrath it seemed beautiful in its simplicity. We would give a party of such magnificence, such opulence, such generosity of spirit and spirits that these poor girls would see the error of their ways, appreciate the superiority of the *Pollack*'s men over these fiancés of theirs, and forthwith return to life as it used to be.

Each of us drew our full liquor ration in champagne for the occasion.

Champagne was not the common staple for officers. Bourbon and Scotch were the favorite drinks, and the allotments were reasonably generous. Ours, which had been accumulating during the entire five months we were on patrol, were monumental. It took about two hundred pounds of ice to surround all our bottles of champagne when they were laid out in a bathtub at the Royal Hawaiian in preparation for the big event.

We called the girls at the Hale Wahine and told them we were coming out to celebrate their engagements. As part of the plan to demonstrate our own superiority, we made sure that all the fiancés would be present. Then we loaded our champagne into a jeep and headed for the Hale. It took two trips to get all the bottles there.

From the first, it was evident that things were not going

as we had planned. Even to our own ears, we sounded a little too loud; the girls of the Hale Wahine seemed mildly embarrassed, and their fiancés showed a tendency to stand off in a scornful little group of their own. Desperately, we opened more bottles of champagne, sang a little louder, recalled more gaily the events of the past when the men of the *Pollack* had looked upon this wonderful house as their own.

Disaster came in the form of a chain reaction. The youngest and fairest of the Wahines suddenly turned green, pressed her handkerchief to her mouth, and fled. Within minutes every other girl in the house had followed her, each looking deathly ill. There was a long pause in the big room, while the fiancés stared bleakly at their hosts. Then the chain reaction resumed.

It had not occurred to us that our lavish outpouring of champagne would be too much for the sweet, proper girls of the Hale Wahine. Even less had we considered the effect on men who had gone for long weeks with no form of strong drink at all, let alone champagne. But, while the little cluster of affianced men watched in disdain, every man jack from the *Pollack* got sick.

Meanwhile, my high hopes of being ordered home to new construction had been dashed again. Lewellen brought me the news. I must make another patrol on the *Pollack*, but when it was done, my turn would surely come. All the hopes I had unwisely built up went glimmering again, and I had to write to Ann that our reunion would be delayed still longer. But this time, I assured her, there could be no doubt about it. After six war patrols I was going to get home one way or another.

My growing self-pity expanded farther at the thought of my old shipmates on the *Wahoo* enjoying themsleves back in the States during their overhaul period and at word of the increasing numbers of my classmates who were being sent back to become execs of new submarines. I ran into one of them, Joe Icenhower, who was on temporary duty waiting orders for new construction. Joe was later to become skipper of the *Jallao*, on which he would finish off a damaged Japanese light cruiser on his first patrol. But even as I envied him, I heard news that shocked me back into a more proper sense of perspective. The Navy announced the loss of the *Triton*, on which my friend Jack Crutchfield had been serving. The *Triton* was one of the war's earliest pacesetters. It had been patrolling off Wake when the Japanese struck, and on December 8, 1941, it had made the first torpedo attack by a Pacific Fleet submarine, damaging an unidentified Japanese warship off Wake. Since then it had sunk eleven Japanese vessels, including a destroyer and a submarine. The thought of Jack and the others who would never return home made me realize how petty my own disappointment was by comparison.

Nevertheless, when the *Pollack* slipped out of Pearl Harbor late in July on her eighth and most eventful war patrol, my attitude was far from what an executive officer's should be. The thought of home and family had become almost an obsession with me. I felt fiercely aggressive, but only because the sooner we expended our torpedoes the sooner we would return from patrol. Meanwhile I fumed, grew a Van

Dyke, listened moodily to Sibelius on the *Pollack*'s record player, and acquired a reputation for a bad temper.

Zully felt the effects of it most. Because I liked him but resented his constant good humor, I found myself riding him unmercifully. The day I caught him cheating on the funny papers I really gave him hell.

On the *Wahoo*'s third patrol, Dick O'Kane had sprung a pleasant surprise that I had carried over to the *Pollack* later as a morale booster. He had brought aboard a big stack of Sunday comics which his wife had saved for him over a period of months, and at specified intervals he would issue a single set. I had written to Ann to ask her to start saving the funnies for me, and the *Pollack* left on its eighth patrol with enough of them to see us through a long trip if they were properly rationed. But we were hardly under way when I caught Zully with a copy two weeks ahead of schedule. His explanation that he simply couldn't stand the suspense of waiting to see what happened to Dick Tracy failed to move me, and the rest of the patrol I kept the comics under lock and key, guarding them as a man might guard drinking water on a raft.

We were headed for the Bungo Suido area, off the Japanese Empire — as the Japanese home islands were universally known in the armed services — at the southern entrance to the Inland Sea. Four days out of Pearl we topped off in Midway — topping off means to fill your fuel tanks to the very top — and set a course for Sofu Gan, the famous dot sticking up out of the Pacific that is commonly known as Lot's Wife.

It was my private hope we would run into a convoy, fire

all our fish, and return before we ever reached our area. But it was nearly two weeks after we left Midway before we sighted our first quarry and launched an attack that almost finished us instead of the enemy.

It was a convoy of two freighters, nearly seven miles away when we first sighted them on a clear August morning. We waited until they were out of sight and then surfaced to chase them. Then, after all the days of inaction, we were suddenly presented an embarrassment of targets. As we followed the two freighters, we sighted a three-ship convoy on a different course still farther in the distance.

We changed targets and began maneuvering to get ahead of the new convoy. Shortly after noon, we were ready. We dived and began a submerged approach on the leading freighter, the biggest of the three. But just as we were ready to fire he zigged toward us, leaving us about three hundred yards off the track. We turned away hastily and fired our two stern tubes. Both missed, and we were swinging to the left to fire at the second freighter with our bow tubes when a depth charge exploded near us.

We had gone below periscope depth for the turn. Now we came up high enough to see what was happening, and found ourselves about six hundred yards ahead of the second freighter. A sudden blast of steam rose in the still air above it — clearly a whistle signal. Captain Lewellen took a quick turn with the periscope and found the answer to the puzzle. There was a destroyer on our starboard quarter, moving in rapidly, so down we went.

Somehow we escaped him. Forty-five minutes later we came up for a periscope look, found ourselves in a clear sea.

and surfaced to give chase. It was after ten o'clock that night before we were back into position for a surface attack, and another hour and a half before we fired all four bow tubes at the largest freighter.

We never knew what they did to him, for at that moment we were flung into a crisis as mysterious as any the temperamental old *Pollack* had ever managed. I was standing in the control room with our most valuable stop watch in my hand, clocking the torpedo run, when a tremendous explosion suddenly shook the boat from one end to the other. It was like no depth charge I had ever experienced. I tossed the stop watch over my shoulder, convinced we were done for and feeling that I didn't want to go to my doom with a stop watch in my hand.

Startled shouts sounded from the bridge. The sea was strangely illuminated all around us. Men were knocked off their feet in the afterpart of the boat and the main contactors were jarred out, causing us to lose all power instantly. We coasted almost to a dead stop.

At that moment, as we sat helpless on the surface, we could have been finished off by almost anything that came along, but fortunately the convoy was as scared as we were. It boiled off over the horizon while we stumbled back into action, made repairs, and finally regained our power. When we did, we picked up the chase again, but the long and fruitless day's efforts, topped off by that stupendous blast, had exhausted us physically and emotionally. Instead of another night surface attack we decided on a submerged periscope attack, and dived ahead of the convoy shortly before daylight. It, in turn, made a radical change in course and escaped us.

Exactly what caused the explosion we never knew, but from long acquaintance with the *Pollack* and her ways we could guess. One of our torpedoes, instead of going toward the target, must have gone straight down and exploded beneath us.

For another two weeks we patrolled the Carolines without incident, then set our course for the Bungo Suido area in the Inland Sea. And there, several days later, our old submarine treated us to the most chilling experience of all.

Shortly after midnight we turned toward a wisp of smoke and found ourselves on the track of a convoy of six ships, apparently four large freighters and two small ones. We were approaching land and the moon was rising, a combination of factors that called for unusual caution. We let the first two freighters go by, then looked the remaining four over and chose the second as the biggest game. The last two ships in formation could not yet be made out, but we thought they were small freighters. In order to get in on the target, we had to get dead ahead of these two, as they were on its quarter.

We were almost in firing position when it became apparent that the nearer of the last two ships was no freighter at all, but a destroyer, and that we would soon be dead ahead of him at only about three thousand yards. It was too late now to change the plan of attack, so we went on in and fired our four bow tubes at the freighter at a range of twenty-five hundred yards. By this time the destroyer was painfully close, though he had evidently not seen us up until the moment we fired.

We went to emergency speed and turned, to put him

astern. As we turned we heard one explosion and saw a column of water shoot up alongside the target. Sound reported a second explosion. We headed away at flank speed, with the destroyer only fifteen hundred yards away and coming in fast. And now it developed that the last ship in column was not a freighter either, but a small escort which had closed in to fourteen hundred yards on our starboard quarter.

We were being mousetrapped. The freighter was sinking, but the two warships were closing in on us at high speed. Taking a page from Mush Morton's book, we tried two down-the-throat shots from our stern tubes at the destroyer. Both missed, and he began shooting at us.

Then, suddenly, our bridge was bathed in brilliant light. He had turned a searchlight on us. Naked under its glare as the two escorts closed on us, we did the only thing possible — we dived at flank speed.

When a submarine is on the surface, the bow planes are rigged in, nestling against the hull and out of water. They must be rigged out by the bow planesman as the boat starts under, tilting to control the depth and angle of dive. The stern planes, which are under water even on the surface and are always rigged out, perform a similar function. But now, as we dived at maximum speed, about eighteen knots, the bow planes refused to rig out and the stern planes jammed on hard dive.

Dives are usually made at a down angle of eight or ten degrees. With that angle and its negative buoyancy, a submarine can get under in a hurry. But now we were about to learn what speed in descent really was. At eighteen knots, with our stern planes immovably fixed on hard dive and our bow planes completely out of the picture, we began to take an angle that was positively incredible.

Down, down, down we went, our speed dangerously high, our angle increasing every second. The depth gauge swung around with chilling speed. We reached our test depth, the depth below which it is considered unsafe to go, and plunged still deeper. Even before we had reached test depth our bow was too deep, for the depth gauge is amidships, a hundred and fifty feet aft of the bow.

The Japanese destroyer above us was dropping depth charges, but no one had time to worry about that. The *Pollack* was headed for suicide on her own. We had to bring her to a stop, or it wouldn't matter whether the depth charges hit or not.

"Blow all main ballast!"

This only made matters worse. The air rushed aft, making the stern lighter and the angle still greater.

By now no one could stand anywhere aboard the *Pollack* without support. Men were hanging on to hatches, tables, controls. Some could not even keep their feet from swinging wildly in the air. The noise was terrific. A submarine's equipment is stored for a reasonable down angle, but this angle was utterly beyond the bounds of reason. All over the boat a roar like summer thunder sounded as equipment fell or dropped or poured out of its storage spaces.

It was the voice of Joe Phelps, our assistant engineering officer, that brought a note of sanity back to the scene.

"For God's sake, Captain," Joe yelled, "ain't it about time to back?"

That was it, an old axiom that Lewellen and I both had forgotten for a moment: when the down angle gets too steep, back and pray.

"All back emergency!" the captain roared. Somehow in the confusion the order got back to the maneuvering room.

The angle indicator had long since gone off its maximum scale of twenty-five degrees down. How far beyond that we were no one knew, and at the moment no one had time to speculate. If we went much deeper, the *Pollack* would collapse like a punctured football. Our only hope was that the backing of the propellers would gradually slow our downward rush.

And slowly, slowly, they began to do it. The *Pollack* lost speed. The angle began to level off. Our feet began to feel steadier beneath us. At last, the *Pollack* came almost to a full stop.

A fresh emergency developed. Our main ballast tanks were almost dry, having been blown in the futile attempt to lighten the *Pollack* enough to slow her down. But now that she had stopped, she was suddenly far too light. The wild ride began in reverse, and we shot upward, right under the Japanese destroyer.

For a while we thought we would break water like a sailfish, but somehow, by venting the tanks and using all our speed, we got the old submarine under control and she came to a reluctant halt just below the surface, and just under the destroyer's keel.

We had gone down about two hundred feet below our test depth, at raging speed and an impossible angle. We had come up the same way. After this, none of us could find the energy to be appropriately concerned over the destroyer. Somehow we escaped her depth charges, moving warily to a lower depth and staying under until daylight. We came up then for a breath of air, and submerged again for the day. All day long we heard the sound of depth charges exploding as the destroyer looked for us, but we were philosophical about it. If we could survive the *Pollack's* own antics, we were too tough for enemy warships to hurt.

It was during that day of submerged exhaustion that we discovered what our dive angle had been the night before. It happened because somebody discovered oil in the coffee.

In the middle of the crew's mess is an overhead vent, hydraulically operated, with a little drip pan welded to it to catch any oil that might drip out. Against the forward bulkhead is a battery of Silex coffee makers. The oil from the drip pan had spilled, pouring into one of the coffee makers. It was a relatively simple matter to figure out our down angle from these factors. We had been headed downward at an angle of fifty-three degrees.

A week later we sank another freighter and took a long and methodical depth-charging from its escort, but this time the *Pollack* behaved herself and we hardly minded. By September 12, we were back at Midway for refueling, and four days later we arrived in Pearl. On the way in, I had ample opportunity to admire the prerogatives of command. The skipper and I played chess often in his stateroom, a space about the size of a bathroom on a Pullman car. The only illumination he would allow in it was a dark red light. We played with red and black pieces on a red and black board, and as the captain, he was entitled to choose his pieces. He always chose the black ones. I had never realized before how maddeningly effective color camouflage can be.

I returned to Pearl in a state of happy anticipation no serviceman should ever allow himself. This time, after all the disappointments and delays, I *knew* I was going home. Lewellen might try to hold me for a couple of days to indoctrinate my replacement, I thought, but I would even talk him out of that. After all, I had not held Gus Weinel more than five minutes when I took over from him. And after six successive patrols, in every one of which contacts had been made with the enemy, I felt frankly incapable of going out again without more than the customary two weeks' rest between patrols. Anything other than immediate orders home to new construction, I told myself, was out of the question.

But it wasn't, of course. Lew came back from his visit to headquarters with the news. Zully and another of our officers, Kenny Ruiz, were going on thirty days' leave. I would remain aboard the *Pollack* until their return; then I would be detached and ordered to the submarine base at Pearl, where I would spend my time refitting submarines returning from patrols.

"It's not as bad as it sounds," Lewellyn told me sympathetically. "You'll be living easy here at Pearl, and after you've been on the job awhile you'll be in good position to be ordered back to new construction when they ask for nominations. When you do go back, you'll be sure of getting thirty days' leave."

There was an alternative, he pointed out. I could ask for a ten-day leave, and probably get it. If I was lucky in transportation, I could spend a few days of it with Ann. But if I did, I'd be dropped from the list of possible nominees for new construction, and fester on the beach at Pearl for about six months before being sent out as commanding officer of an old submarine. And after *that*, there would be no hope of getting home for another year or more.

It was too little, after all my expectations. I turned it down bitterly, wrote a long, angry letter to Ann, and prepared to make the worst of it. The thought that other men have stayed out longer and suffered worse is no consolation to a man disappointed in his hopes for a leave. The tendency is to think instead of men who have got home sooner after enduring less. Again the fortunes of war had brought my brother John and me to Pearl at the same time; I went over to his ship to get him and we went out and got thoroughly drunk to celebrate my misfortune.

10
New Construction

I HAD BARELY SETTLED into my new routine when the good news came. On October 21, four or five months before I had any reason to expect them, my orders arrived. I was to report on January 3 to Manitowoc, Wisconsin, where the new submarine *Hawkbill* was being built, and I could probably count on a thirty-day leave en route.

It meant that, with any luck at all, I would be home by Christmas. A little shamefaced over my late bitterness, I wrote Ann a jubilant letter, telling her to start buying winter clothes and to prepare herself for an idyllic winter in Wisconsin. For almost a month more I did odd jobs on the *Pollack*, which was taking part in training exercises for antisubmarine ships at Pearl, and then I was detached and sent over to the Navy Yard to arrange transportation.

In those days, the chances of getting a quick trip back to the West Coast were slim. You usually had to wait around until some Army or Navy transport pulled out and you could ride in the bilges. There was the Pan-American

Clipper, of course, but you had to be practically an admiral even to be considered for a ride on it. However, I thought there would be no harm in going around to the officer in charge of air transportation, just to try. And now it seemed that fate, which had frowned on me so recently, could not do enough for me. When I walked into the air-transportation office late in November, 1943, who should be sitting behind the desk but an old neighbor of Ann's and mine from the prewar days in Honolulu.

The Clipper took off two days later. On board were four admirals, two or three captains, an assortment of miscellaneous VIPs, and one nervous lieutenant commander named Grider. It was a great trip, with stewards bowing and smiling and all kinds of luxuries I had almost forgotten, and it got me to San Francisco in twenty-four hours.

I took the plane down to Burbank, and there stood my lovely wife. After all the hopes and disappointments, there was an awkward quality about our meeting. It seemed unreal, like an encounter in a dream, to step off a plane and see her before me at last. For a few moments, as we groped to renew the intimate bonds of communication, we were like strangers.

We drove back to Long Beach to pick up Billy and then went across country to Memphis for a Christmas I shall never forget. Then, secure in the knowledge that we had months of happiness still before us, we drove up to Manitowoc, where the *Hawkbill* was being built.

I don't think anyone did a better job building submarines during the war than the people in Manitowoc. There was a large number of old German artisans at the Manitowoc Shipbuilding Company, men who had been building lake steamers for years. They had developed techniques for building submarines that were completely new. They built them in sections and then welded the sections together, turning the submarine like a roast on a spit, and doing all the welding from above. And then, when they got it assembled parallel to the river, on the dock, they just pushed it into the water sideways to launch it. I am not sure, but I believe submarines were the biggest ships that were launched sideways at that time. At any rate, I know that among those artisans who had been building subs during two wartime years, the supervisory job of the officers was far simpler than it had been during those hectic months when we had watched the *Wahoo* take shape at Mare Island.

We had a wonderful time in Manitowoc. The people there were good to us. My new captain was Worth Scanland, a man of whom I was very fond and a very able and efficient naval officer. He had the tradition more deeply than I. His father had had command of the *Nevada* at Pearl Harbor, had got her under way and stood halfway out of the harbor on the day of the attack before he had to put her aground because of torpedo holes in her. Worth had grown up in the Navy, and he loved it.

The senior submarine officer at Manitowoc, in general charge of the three or four subs that were always in the process of being built, was Bull Wright, my old friend of the *Sturgeon*, a man who had turned in a magnificent fighting record since his memorable report in the early days of the war, "STURGEON NO LONGER VIRGIN." Bull was not only a great fighter and an able administrator, but a fine storyteller as well. He used to regale us at Manitowoc with the story of how he had directed Reuben Whitaker, his exec, to "take care of it" when Reuben tried to wake him with the news we were at war with Japan. And he had a fine story to tell about one of his mess boys.

This boy was an excellent lookout, Bull said, but as skipper he felt it never hurt to impress a sailor with his responsibilities. One night the *Sturgeon* had surfaced so near Honshu that you could almost see the Japanese on it. The mess attendant had come up for the midwatch, cleaned off his glasses, and begun a sweep of the horizon, and when he saw Honshu, it was clear he was a trifle unnerved. Bull had been watching him. "Now, son," he said gravely, "you know that you're a good lookout, and you've got to stand your watch properly. There's a lot of men down below whose lives depend on the way you stand this watch." The boy nodded and swallowed. "That's right, sir," he gulped. "And then there's me, too."

Living quarters at Manitowoc were limited, and we lived in what was almost a shack, but life was unforgettably pleasant after the strenuous months of combat. I had never been as tired as I was during the final days of my last war patrol on the *Pollack*, and it was indescribable luxury to relax and live what seemed an almost normal life again. While we were there my classmates began to get command of their own submarines, and I was offered an opportunity to go back out to the Pacific and get a command then and there. But I knew the war still had a long way to go; I had been with the *Hawkbill* long enough to feel needed; I liked her officers and was sure she was going to make a good record; and I thought it would do me good to make one more patrol as an executive officer. Aside from all these excellent reasons, of course, was the overpowering one that I did not want to cut short my stay with my wife and child.

The *Hawkbill* was commissioned about the middle of May, and tested for a couple of weeks in Lake Michigan. It was a strange sensation to dive in fresh water. It had never occurred to me there would be any difference, but there was. For one thing, we learned to our surprise that in fresh water the radio worked just as well at deep submergence as it did on the surface, whereas in salt water it became virtually useless when we went deep. For another, we were unable to use one of our standard tests for a leak. In the Pacific, if anyone saw water on the deck or oozing through a seam when we were submerged, he tasted it. If it was salty, he knew the boat had sprung a leak; otherwise, it was all right. It took us a long time to get used to the idea that this was no good in Lake Michigan. And it was strange, too, to come in from a run on the lake with ice caked on the deck. That was something else we had not encountered in the South Pacific.

Finally we set out. We went to Chicago under our own power and were towed through the Chicago Drainage Canal. Then, at Lockport, Illinois, the *Hawkbill* was put in a sort of floating drydock to be pushed down the river to New Orleans. I didn't make the trip down the river with her. In a way I have always regretted it, because it would have been wonderful to sit on the deck and read Mark Twain's *Life on the Mississippi*. But it was a choice of riding the boat down the river or driving to New Orleans with my family, and Mark Twain ran a poor second. So we left the *Hawkbill* at Lockport and set out for Memphis on June 6. We were hardly on our way before the radio began blaring the news of D day in Europe, and all the way we listened to the accounts of the Normandy landings. With another farewell ahead of us, it was an especially encouraging and exciting thing to know a milestone had been reached in the European war.

We reached Memphis ahead of the *Hawkbill*, and I made arrangements with the Coast Guard to take me and my guardian, Wilson Northcross, aboard her. Wilson had looked out for the Griders since my father's death in World War I, and had worried over Ann like a father in the days when I was at Marc Island and she was nursing her dying mother in Memphis. I felt that somehow he would relish a closer look at the kind of craft that was keeping me away from home.

The Coast Guard people told us we had to be off the *Hawkbill*'s floating drydock and on our way back to shore before the new sub went below the bridge just south of Memphis's business district, because their jurisdiction ended there and for some wartime reason they had to leave the ship there. So Wilson and Sam Nickey, another old friend, and I went out as the tug reached Memphis and climbed aboard the drydock and up the *Hawkbill*'s side to stand on her deck. I thought there would be time to go below, so I herded them toward the after torpedo-room hatch. On the way down, Wilson got his knee caught under one rung of the ladder and his instep caught in another, and was firmly stuck. He hung there for several minutes as we approached the bridge, and for a while I wondered if he would have to make the first war patrol with us, hung in the afterhatch like the torpedo that was jammed in its tube during the first patrol of the *Wahoo*. We got him free in time to satisfy the Coast Guard.

We had a glorious farewell period for four or five days in New Orleans. Sam Nickey and his wife drove down with Ann and me; the wives or sweethearts of all the other officers were there; and we found my old Naval Academy roommate, Bill Wendel, was stationed in New Orleans in command of a blimp. Bill had gone back to civilian life after our days at the Academy and had returned to the Navy for the war. His blimp was assigned to escort us into the Gulf after we left New Orleans.

In those final days ashore I learned to appreciate our officers even more than I had at Manitowoc. They were a wonderful bunch. Fred Tucker, who was later to save the *Hawkbill* on her fifth patrol by getting her out of shallow water after she had been depth-charged and knocked to the surface, was the third officer. There were Gale Christopher and Lou Fockele and Jack Jackson, who had been with me on the *Pollack*, and Eric Schroeder and an ensign named Rex Murphy, one of the most solid citizens I ever knew. We would need him soon, to face the crisis of the sanitary tank. But now all of us made merry in New Orleans, until the time came to say good-by.

Bill Wendel and his blimp set out ahead of us when we departed on June 16, but he didn't stay ahead for long. He kept trying to bring the blimp down close enough to drop a line on our afterdeck, and instead of staying up ahead and looking for submarines, he spent most of his time astern, sending insulting messages to me by blinker, all of which I answered in kind. But in a way I suppose it was good escorting. If any U-boats had been lurking off the mouth of the river that afternoon, they would probably have been afraid to attack because of our peculiar maneuvers.

Our first destination was the submarine base at Balboa in the Canal Zone, and even before we reached it, we were abruptly reminded that we were once more part of a nation at war. As we were going through the Yucatan Channel, between Cuba and Mexico, we were fired on by a merchant ship of undetermined nationality.

Worth Scanland saw it first. The ship was about eight miles away when Worth saw the flash of his guns. He turned to the lookout and said, "Keep a sharp watch about two miles off our port beam." The lookout returned a casual "Aye, aye, sir," and then nearly fell off the bridge in amazement when shells hit about a couple of miles away. Worth waited until the ship fired a few more rounds, and then we got out our big signal searchlight and sent him a message, "CEASE FIRING." He promptly ceased.

At Balboa we paused for a training period with many torpedo runs, and our record for accuracy turned out to be even better than it should have been, at least in two cases when I was making the runs. Our training torpedoes had dummy warheads on them, and they were set to go under their targets. But on the day I made my first approach and fired at the poor destroyer that spent its entire life running practice runs for submarines, something went wrong with the depth-control mechanism. The torpedo ran right below the surface, hit the destroyer, and crashed through into the engine room. The destroyer straggled into port, got patched up, and came out about three days later. I made another run, and, by heaven, the same thing happened again. Two holes in the side of a friendly destroyer before we got to Pearl.

We anchored at night in the Perles Islands, somewhere in the Gulf of Panama on the Pacific side. The Perles were pleasant and quiet. We never got off the boat; we just sat around at night and looked at the moon and fished over the side.

About the middle of July we left for Pearl, where we spent another week or so in really intensive training before topping off to leave on our first patrol. My most vivid memory of that stop in Pearl was a visit with the admiral. We were going to be part of a scouting line in a major fleet action — the sort of thing submarines were expected in prewar days to concentrate on, but something that very rarely happened after combat began — and the skippers and execs of the subs involved were called in for briefing by Admiral Lockwood and his staff in the inner sanctum of the offices of Commander, Submarine Force, Pacific Fleet.

Lockwood explained to us in some detail the Allied plans for a landing in the Philippines and our part in the plans. I was greatly impressed with him. He was an admiral, which alone was enough to impress me, but beyond that he was competent, thorough, and quite at ease in the responsibilities of his command — a man who inspired and radiated confidence. Remembering his message telling Mush that his picture was on the piano, I felt a fresh pride in serving under this imaginative, daring, and thoroughly human executive. And I was doubly impressed with the weight of the secret information I shared. We were supposed to leave that same day, but something came up that delayed us until the next day, and I was actually afraid to leave the base that night because of the knowledge I had. I stayed on board ship.

There was other big brass in Hawaii about that time, and we on the *Hawkbill* made the most of it. Election day was coming up, and the Navy Department, under the stimulus of Congress, was doing everything possible to encourage participation in it by the men in service. Voluminous instructions had been sent out on the methods to be used to inform the men of their rights, to help them in their efforts to get absentee ballots, and even to instruct them in a nonpartisan way on the issues of the day. This instruction was to be given when the crew was called to quarters.

One day while we were tied up to the dock at the submarine base, word was sent down that one of the members of a top-level conference then under way at Pearl was going to drive through the base. All the subs were to get their crews on deck and man the side, or salute him, as he went by.

The opportunity to combine two directives was too good to miss. I called the *Hawkbill* crew up on deck and got them in formation. They looked rather smart for a submarine crew during the war, which is to say they were all wearing shirts and hats. I gave them the instructions on how to get absentee ballots and made a brief talk about the issues involved in the election. All the while I kept my eye on the road that flanked the dock. As the flurry of activity along it drew nearer, I brought my remarks to a close, and with a sense of timing I have always been proud of, I announced, "And now, in pursuance of the usual service that we render on this boat, I want you to meet one of the candidates."

Turning at that moment, I snapped out an order to salute, and the eyes of every man aboard bugged out as Franklin Delano Roosevelt drove by and waved at us.

Our orders were to leave Pearl, refuel at Saipan, and take station on a scouting line to the east of the Philippines, near San Bernardino Strait. We left on August 23 and moored alongside the *Holland*, one of our old submarine tenders, a week and a half later at Saipan for fuel and minor repairs, and Worth sent me over to a seaplane tender to get some charts. When I went up in the chartroom, met the navigator, and told him what I wanted, he yelled to a tall dark-haired officer in the background, "Say, Hank, go get me such and such charts." I was there for perhaps twenty minutes, and every time the exec wanted something he would call Hank to get it. I was beginning to feel a little sorry for the poor fellow when I got a better look at him and recognized him as Henry Fonda. Years later, when I saw him in *Mr. Roberts*, I was deeply impressed by his portrayal of a mildly harassed Navy officer.

Our great hopes of tangling with the Japanese fleet came to nothing. We patrolled off the eastern approaches to the Philippines throughout the major part of September, dodging planes and watching for the fleet, but it never came our way. Finally we were ordered into an area west of Formosa for a few more days of uneventful patrolling, and then we headed further south into the South China Sea.

There our luck changed.

About seven o'clock one night, just as it was getting dark, we picked up a large freighter and an escort through the high periscope. We were on the surface with the periscope extended to its full height, using it to look for targets completely hidden over the horizon from the bridge. Immediately we began maneuvering to get into position for a night surface attack. Nearly three hours later we were ready and fired four of our electric torpedoes.

A major advantage of the electric torpedoes with which the *Hawkbill* was armed was that they left no wake. A steam torpedo is driven by a combination of air pressure and steam which exhausts out the tail and rises to the surface in the form of little bubbles which leave a wake you can see for miles, but the propeller of an electric torpedo is driven by electricity and makes only a little turbulence in the water, which can't be seen. The advantage, especially when you are attacking an escorted vessel, is obvious.

But on the score of accuracy our torpedoes failed us, or we failed to aim them properly. All four missed, for reasons we were never able to establish. We swung our stern around and fired two more from our after tubes, and these missed too. Even without the wakes to give us away, all this activity inevitably attracted the attention of the escort, and it turned toward us.

It was something smaller and less speedy than a destroyer, and by putting it astern and bending on all our power, we were able to get away. But after spending forty-five days on patrol without one enemy ship to show for it, Worth Scanland was in no mood to give up. After we shook the escort we came in again for another approach, still on the surface, and a little more than half an hour after the first attack we fired three more torpedoes.

These hit, and the fireworks began.

Our first fish hit the afterhold. It was already in flames when the second one hit in the forward hold about ten seconds later. Flames broke out all over the ship, and a series of small explosions sounded.

I was standing on the bridge with Worth when, about a minute after the first torpedo hit, a mighty concussion shook my insides. A wave of heat enveloped me, and at the same moment came the sound of a tremendous explosion. We held on to keep from falling and watched the sight before us with awestruck eyes.

We had hit an ammunition ship, touching off fireworks that made the combined displays of a dozen Fourth of Julys look like a pair of tired lightning bugs by comparison. The entire area was bathed in light. White and yellow flames rose in a vast mushroom hundreds of feet into the air. Rockets and tracer ammunition blazed weird diagrams across the sky as flaming bits of wreckage flew up and fell smoking back into the ocean. We were witnessing the utter disintegration of a large and heavily loaded ship.

Officers from the conning tower crowded up the hatch to look. Worth Scanland was filled with a delight reminiscent of Mush Morton's fierce glee, for he had a brother fighting with the ground troops in Burma, and the instant he had realized this was an ammunition ship, the thought had occurred to him that its cargo might have been intended for use in the very area where his brother was.

As if to add to the pyrotechnic display before us, the escort ship suddenly and unaccountably began firing green rocket submarine-warning signals — even as the remains of the freighter it was charged with protecting disappeared into the water. But in another instant those of us who had laughed at the rockets were abruptly sobered. The escort had begun firing 20-millimeter tracers at us, and the rounds were whizzing over the bridge and threatening our periscope shears. The explosions that we heard now were in the water directly around us. Still Worth did not dive. He called for more speed from the maneuvering room, and slowly we pulled out of range. It was an hour before we breathed safely again.

Shortly after midnight we made another long-range contact. Radar picked up a ship fifteen miles away. We knew it had to be big, and we began tracking. When we got in to a range of about five and a half miles, we could see him clearly through the binoculars — an aircraft carrier, escorted by two destroyers, and making a speed of seventeen knots.

The moon was up, visibility was good, and the sea was fairly rough. Worth called for all the power we had. But it wasn't enough; we could barely keep up with him, and two hours of trying to get into position for attack failed. Evidently he had good radar himself, because every maneuver we made was matched by one of his own which kept us constantly abeam.

It was such a magnificent target and we were so anxious to get it that we almost forgot the destroyers. We corrected the oversight just in time. While the carrier was still five and a half miles away from us, just as he had been two hours before, we suddenly discovered one of the destroyers only three miles away and boiling toward us.

This time there was no choice but to dive. We went down to what was supposed to be deep submergence for the *Hawkbill* and got the most rapid depth-charge attack I was ever in. There were nineteen depth charges, and they went off almost simultaneously. It was so bad that we went down a hundred feet below our test depth to get away. Almost immediately, as soon as he could turn around, the destroyer was back for another salvo, but this was not quite so close. He hung around over us for three hours, pinging and occasionally dropping a depth charge.

None of them came close enough for discomfort, but now we discovered the destroyer had been responsible for one casualty he would never dream of — the malfunction of a valve in the sanitary tank. To explain what this meant, I must first report the wartime progress that had been made in plumbing facilities on submarines.

The old, intricate system of closing Bowl Flapper Valve "A," opening Gate Valve "C," and so on before flushing the head no longer prevailed. On the newer submarines we had an unfamiliar luxury, a rather large tank built into the hull in the forward torpedo room and known as the sanitary tank. The head discharged directly into this tank, at the end of the day the tank was blown once, and that was that. We had blessed its simplicity many times since we first boarded the *Hawkbill*, but now we were to learn that progress had its price.

The sanitary tank was protected from sea pressure by a sea valve. In the event the sea valve leaked, there was a relief valve just above it. Worth Scanland's decision to go below our test depth to escape the depth charges had worked out beautifully, with but one exception. Under the increasing pressure, the sea valve had leaked and built up tremendous pressure in the sanitary tank. Suddenly, about five o'clock in the morning, the relief valve performed its intended function. It lifted and, with a great burst of noise and an indescribably noxious odor, began spraying the contents of the sanitary tank into the forward torpedo room.

I was in the control room when a messenger came dashing in, followed by an aroma, to report that the relief valve had lifted. Within seconds, the control room and the conning tower above us were so permeated with the atmosphere that had followed him that it was unnecessary to repeat his message to Worth above me.

The skipper came reluctantly down the hatch and looked about the control room. His eyes fell on Rex Murphy, our solid, reliable ensign for whom no job had ever been found that was too tough, and whose composure had never faltered.

"Rex," said the captain, averting his eyes, "I want you to wade in there and shut off that valve."

To his everlasting credit, Ensign Murphy uttered no word of protest. "Aye, aye, sir," he said, and took a deep breath, lowered his head, and charged through the miasmic fog into the forward torpedo room. There he waded over to the relief valve and, in the highest traditions of the naval service, grasped it with his hand and shut it.

He had to stand there and hold it shut for about an hour.

It was one of the most valorous acts I witnessed throughout the war, and it is good to report that Murph received special recognition for his feat. Even after he had taken twenty baths within a two-day period, every man and officer aboard honored him on sight with the Murphy Salute — the thumb and forefinger clasped downward over the nose.

We surfaced about eight o'clock after that memorable night, and had no sooner manned the bridge than we sighted the aircraft carrier again and dived in hopes of making a submerged daytime attack. He was only seven miles away now, and without escort, and we spent eight solid hours trying to get into position to fire. But he never steadied down, he never slowed down, and he never allowed us to come in close enough to shoot. At last, about sundown, we lost contact with him completely. We surfaced and resumed the search, but he had disappeared over the horizon and we never saw him again. In a sense, good old Murph's sacrifice had been in vain.

Our orders called for us to leave the area the next afternoon and head for Australia, in company with the *Becuna*, under command of Hank Sturr. Shortly before dawn the *Hawkbill* maneuvered alongside her sister sub, and Worth and Hank stood on their bridges and discussed the situation with the aid of small hand megaphones. It was not an uncommon thing for subs to do when they were operating together, but the sight of those two boats up from the deep, water still dripping off their decks, standing side by side in the dark in enemy waters while their captains exchanged shouted messages, gave me a fresh sense of the strangely unreal quality of submarine warfare in general.

It was decided that the *Becuna* would lead the way by an hour or so as we transited Mindoro Strait. But we had no sooner left the area than the *Becuna* sent us a contact report — a convoy to the north. Within less than half an hour we had picked it up ourselves. This was a big convoy, composed of twelve big ships, tankers and freighters, with three escorts. It was still daylight, so we went down for an attack.

Before we could get into position, we heard torpedo hits

from the *Becuna,* and hell broke loose in the convoy. The ships began altering their courses wildly and the escorts began dropping depth charges. But we were able to line up for attacks on two freighters, firing four torpedoes at the first and two at the second. Between firings, we saw the *Becuna's* tanker sinking, and after firing at our second target, we saw two of our torpedoes hit our first target. We turned the periscope to watch results on the second vessel we had fired at, and just as we saw the first torpedo hit, one of the escorts dropped a depth charge directly under the forward part of the *Hawkbill.*

It was a violent explosion, knocking men down in the forward torpedo room and toppling the operator of the gyro angle regulator off his stool, but damage was slight. Still, we had to give up watching and go deep. In the next two hours we counted ninety-six depth charges. Darkness fell, and Worth, who seemed to feel there was something almost shameful about submergence, brought us back up to start an end-around on the remains of the convoy. There were now three ships missing from it, which indicated Hank Sturr had sunk his and we had sunk or damaged our two. We dogged the convoy until shortly before midnight, finally getting into position and firing three torpedoes at a large passenger freighter. All three escorts were after us now, the convoy was heading into dangerously shallow water, we were out of torpedoes forward and in doubt as to our position, and all hands were exhausted. So, after seeing and hearing one hit on the target and watching a cloud of heavy black smoke blanket the ship, Worth sighed wearily and gave the order to head for Mindoro Strait.

We picked up the masts of another convoy early the next morning, while we were still headed for the strait, and tracked it in broad daylight almost within sight of the Japanese air bases nearby. But, when we were within a few minutes of being in position to dive and attack, an enemy plane spotted us, came over, and dropped a bomb. It didn't do any damage, but it meant we were not going to get in on that convoy.

We entered Mindoro Strait then and went down through the Sulu Sea, through Macassar Strait and Lombok Strait, and finally into the Indian Ocean. Remarkably, we made the entire passage from Mindoro Strait into the Indian Ocean without sighting a Japanese ship or aircraft of any kind, and without submerging. We made it in eighty-one hours, which was fast moving indeed for a submarine in enemy waters.

As we arrived in Perth on October 18, 1944, I was aware of two things. One was the remarkable record of aggressiveness Worth Scanland had made on this first patrol of the *Hawkbill*, evidenced not only by her successful attacks but also by the fact that we had not made one all-day dive during the entire patrol. The other was that my own test of aggressiveness and leadership lay just ahead of me. I was wearing the shoulder boards of a commander now. We had known Worth would make commander during the patrol, and we had bought a hat and shoulder boards to surprise him with when the orders came in. Then, on the same day his promotion arrived, mine did too, and I got the shoulder boards. The next time I went out on patrol, I knew now beyond doubt, it would be as captain of my own submarine.

II

Command

THERE WAS NO CITY in the world like Perth for submarine men, especially in that fall of 1944 when our subs were at a staggering peak of effectiveness against the Japanese navy and merchant marine. Admiral Ralph W. Christie, Commander of Submarines, Southwest Pacific, saw to that. Perth was his headquarters and the base for his men between patrols, and if ever an admiral saw to the welfare of his men, Admiral Christie did.

There were virtually no other troops at Perth, for it was neither an air base nor an army base. Christie's squadrons operated from a tender tied up to the dock at Fremantle, the port of Perth, and aside from the crews of a few British subs, we had the city to ourselves. Christie worked on the theory that the way to make submarine men efficient was to give them a luxurious life when they were recuperating, and he spared no pains to see that we had it. Each submarine, as it arrived from patrol, was assigned a couple of automobiles, one for the enlisted men and the other for the officers. The men had a hotel that was all theirs, the junior officers had another, and the captains had a couple of bungalows in a beautiful residential area known as Birdwood.

And the girls were everywhere. The Aussies take a more austere view than we do of how to fight a war: all their men had gone off in 1939 and had not been back since. There were many, many girls and war wives in Perth, and no able-bodied men except the submariners. The automobiles assigned to the subs were invariably chauffeured by attractive girls during the daylight hours. There were beautiful girls at the clubs, in the stores, on the streets, and romance was everywhere. I don't know how many submariners under Admiral Christie's command married Aussie girls, but the number must have been impressive.

Rumblings of discontent had already begun to sound from North Africa, as Aussie soldiers learned the scope of this peaceful invasion. Some enterprising newspaperman had run a series of interviews with the women of Perth, centering around one loaded question: "Why do you prefer Americans to Aussies?" The girls had replied in public print that the Americans were a great deal more polite, that they stood up when a lady entered the room, that they lit her cigarettes and sent flowers to her and treated her generally with fine romantic feeling. When the home-town newspapers reached those poor Aussie soldiers who had been sweating on the desert for so long, the effect can well be imagined. A feeling about Americans — and submariners in particular — developed among western Australian servicemen overseas that was downright bitter. I for one was inclined to respect it, then and later. I remember that shortly after the war when I was on a train in the United States, in uniform, I came across four Aussies in the club car. In the conversation that followed, it developed all four of them were from Perth. They could tell from my insignia that I was a submariner. After a while one of them asked me, with elaborate unconcern, whether I had ever been in Perth. The others tensed noticeably as they waited for my answer. I looked them all in the eye and shook my head. "No," I said regretfully, "I've never been to Perth."

The word of my new orders had come even sooner than I expected — before we went ashore at Fremantle, in fact. When we tied up to the *Euryale,* our submarine tender, Admiral Christie came aboard and shook hands all around, and after he had talked to Worth a while, he looked at me. "Grider," he said, "you're going to take command of the *Flasher.*"

The *Flasher* was the hottest submarine then operating out of Perth, and my elation was matched only by my misgivings as to whether I could maintain her pace. My old friend and fellow Memphian, Reuben Whitaker, had built her into a magnificent fighting machine. Since January she had been credited with sinking no fewer than fourteen Japanese vessels, all the way from a river gunboat to a light cruiser, a transport, and some cargo ships of tremendous tonnage. It was a record that would stand up, after all the claims had been sifted and compared with the Japanese records, as one of the best of the entire war. Now, after taking the *Flasher* out on four consecutive patrols, Reuben was to get a rest. He was going back to New London to teach at the Submarine School. The prospect of taking command of this fine boat from so great a warrior and friend was more than I had hoped for.

As prospective commanding officer, I was assigned to Birdwood, and, as the hour approached toward which my entire naval career had been fashioned, I settled into a brief period of life as idyllic as can be imagined during a war. We were awakened each morning by a houseboy who handed us glasses of orange juice, a luxury exceedingly dear in Australia at the time. A luxurious breakfast would follow, consisting of many delicacies in addition to the standard drink served at all meals and in between all meals, the glorious Australian beer in quart bottles. Then would come an utterly relaxed and carefree day.

Birdwood usually housed about twelve skippers. We would loaf through the mornings or go on picnics with civilian friends — a few older married couples and several young ladies were usually available to help make the days pleasant — and later we would have dances or play silly games or sit around and talk. That was the first place I ever saw the Hokey-Pokey. The dance was then the rage in Australia, and all of us had to learn to "do the Hokey-Pokey."

For a man about to assume command, the atmosphere beneath the surface was both stimulating and challenging. All about me were men who had done great deeds and would go on to greater ones. Herm Kossler of the *Cavalla*, who had just sunk one of the three largest Japanese aircraft carriers in commission, was in the room next to mine. Bob Madison of the *Mingo* was nearby, just back from a dramatic lifeguard operation in the waters off Borneo. The *Mingo* had rescued sixteen Liberator pilots from land or water after a Thirteenth Air Force Liberator strike, and had been bombed by a Liberator by mistake on the run back. Bob had brought back a native dugout, used by one of the fliers he rescued, as a present for the Officers' Club in Fremantle.

My old friend and classmate Chester Nimitz, Jr., left the night I arrived. Chester had just been relieved as captain of the *Haddo*, on which he had sunk five Japanese ships within a thirty-day period during his past patrol. He was going back to the States on leave before returning to take a desk assignment, much against his will, on Admiral Christie's staff. He left his golf bags with me and warned me that the admiral was an enthusiastic golfer.

Frank Hayler, Fran Greenup, and Ben Oakley also were preparing to leave Perth as the *Hawkbill* arrived. Oakley, on the *Growler*, was in command of a wolfpack that included Hayler's *Hake* and Greenup's *Hardhead*. It was the last time we were to see Oakley — the *Growler* was lost at sea soon afterward — but in only a few weeks I would see Fran Greenup at a time when I urgently needed him.

They came and went as we rested: Pinky Baer of the *Lapon*, just back from a patrol on which two cargo ships and a tanker had been sunk; Jack Martin of the *Hammerhead*, who had sent five ships to the bottom during October; and other fine skippers, like Si Austin of the *Redfin*, J. P. Fitzpatrick of the *Paddle*, Dave Bell of the *Pargo*, and Vic McCrea of the *Hoe*.

And before we left, two more crews arrived with one of the most dramatic stories of the year. They came doubled up in a single submarine. Dave McClintock of the *Darter* and Ike Claggett of the *Dace* had gone out as a team under McClintock's command to work between northeast Borneo and the area known, for good cause, as the Dangerous Grounds off Palawan. They had run into the main body of the Imperial Second Fleet, headed for Palawan to contest MacArthur's landing at Leyte. The *Dace* had sunk the heavy cruiser *Maya*. The *Darter* had blasted the Japanese admiral's flagship, the heavy cruiser *Atago*, crippled another heavy cruiser, and then run aground in a perilous attempt to get in for a killer shot in shallow water. Claggett had taken his boat to the aid of the helpless *Darter* and rescued its entire crew, which was now about to be sent back to the States as a unit to take over a new submarine.

With men like these coming and going about me, I found myself alternately exulting in the reflection of their glory and caught up in sudden doubts that I could ever match their aggressive spirits when I went out on my own. It is one thing to be an executive officer and an entirely different thing to be the man one step higher, who must make the final decisions. I went to sleep often in a turmoil of introspection.

Meanwhile, there were lighter stories to listen to, like Fran Greenup's version of how he had found Bunky Bakutis. Bunky was an aviator, an old friend of Greenup's, and he had been in an air strike and strafed a Japanese battleship. As he passed over, the guns of the escort on the far side found him, and he went down in the Sulu Sea miles and miles from land. Bunky, a hard man to panic, blew up his little one-man life raft and floated around in it two or three days. One night the *Hardhead* happened along en route to its patrol station. It was a dark night, and the officer of the deck was dubious when the lookout told him he thought they had just passed a small boat. But the radar operator picked it up, too, so they made a pass at Bunky's raft. By this time, Fran was on the bridge. There wasn't a sign of life from the raft, but they turned and made another pass, and this time they hailed it. Bunky yelled back, "American aviator. Come over and pick me up." Fran was startled by the casual, familiar tone, and took another look. "Bunky!" he roared. "What the hell are you doing out here?" And Bunky, with a great air of goodwill, called back, "Hel-*lo*, Francis!" So they picked him up and transferred him to Frank Hess's *Angler* the next morning for a ride back to Perth. What delighted Greenup was the reason Bunky hadn't hailed them the first time they passed: there he was, floating around in a hostile ocean, soundly and peacefully asleep.

There was an Aussie Commando there, too, known as Wild Bill Jenkins. He was a lone wolf in the war. The subs would take him to Borneo or some other enemy-held island and put him ashore, and he would spend two or three months making contacts with the rebels and stirring up what trouble he could before arranging a rendezvous by radio. A sub would pick him up at the appointed spot and bring him back to Perth to get ready for another patrol. He talked about his exploits in the same matter-of-fact way a housewife might discuss a trip to the grocery store.

The admiral had me in for lunch and asked if I would like to play a round of golf. I had never been a good golfer, but in my present state of exhilaration I felt nothing could stop me. I rushed back to Birdwood for the clubs Chester had lent me and returned to take on the admiral. As it turned out, it was a good thing he did not judge his skippers by their golfing ability. He was very good and I was terrible. The course was built on the side of a mountain, and in my old GI shoes I couldn't even climb the fairways without slipping back. I shot something like a 175 and considered myself lucky indeed that my promised orders to command the *Flasher* came through in spite of it.

During the next few days, while Reuben Whitaker waited to be relieved officially of his command, he and I held frequent bull sessions in front of the fire at our Birdwood cottage and he briefed me on the *Flasher* and her officers. Then, on the last day of October, I relieved him, put him on the plane for home, and went aboard the *Flasher* to try to grow accustomed to the sensation of being called "Captain." It was all I could do to keep a silly grin off my face every time I heard the word.

My executive officer was Phil Glennon, a thorough and efficient lad who had fallen in love with a delightful Aussie girl and hoped to marry her after the next patrol. Snap Coffin was the engineer and third officer. After them came Tom Burke, Mac McCants, Kiko Harrison, Jim Hamlin, and our one ensign, Eddie Atkinson. All of them had been on at least one patrol on the *Flasher*, and Reuben had commended them to me highly. And, as we began to warm up to one another, I found myself in enthusiastic agreement.

It was strange to realize, as every new captain must, that these men were actually a little afraid of me at first, just as

Roger Paine and I and all the others had been a little afraid of Mush Morton when he first took over the *Wahoo*. After all, I was an unknown factor, and their safety as well as their effectiveness depended on me. I made a studied attempt, in the days of training exercises that followed, to be casual in everything I did and to appear unconcerned in emergencies. Once, as we were turning around in the Swan River at Fremantle, I deliberately let the *Flasher* slip back almost into the torpedo net, timing my "All ahead two thirds" so that she pulled away about a yard before the screws tangled in the net. It was intended to demonstrate a great faculty for composure, but Phil told me later it worried hell out of the officers.

We learned one another's ways for six days while we conducted training exercises and fired a couple of dummy torpedoes. Then, on November 15, the *Flasher* set out on her fifth war patrol, and for the first time I was face to face with the awesome responsibility of command.

Every man who ever got command of any ship must have gone through the same period of adjustment that I did on the *Flasher*. In every other wartime situation in which I had found myself, no matter how much reliance might have been placed on me, I had known there was someone nearby who had to make the final decision and assume the final responsibility. I had become conditioned to the idea of calling the captain in any emergency. Now, suddenly, there was no one to call but me. It was a glorious feeling to stand on the bridge and look at the *Flasher* and know she was all mine, but it was also a lonely feeling, and a disquieting one.

We were to travel in company with the *Becuna* and the

Hawkbill for the early part of the patrol. On the *Hawkbill* with Worth Scanland was Captain E. H. Bryant, our wolf-pack commander, who would make general decisions involving our movements as long as we operated in a pack, but when any of us found game, the fight would be our own.

The first week, as we proceeded from Perth up the western coast of Australia, around the Northwest Cape, and into Darwin, was uneventful. We teamed up with the *Hawkbill* for tracking drills, submerged and surface approaches, and tests of new electronic equipment. I was surprised to discover how little there was for the skipper to do, and in a way it was bad for me. It provided too much time for self-analysis. I found myself fretting over a head cold and its possible effects on my aggressiveness. I worried about eating too much, but found it hard to go to sleep without downing a can of peanuts and a candy bar first. When I slept well, I worried about not waking promptly in case of an emergency; when I slept poorly, I worried about the drain on my energy. Eager to get my mind off myself, I launched a patrol-long cribbage match with Phil Glennon and worked overtime at plans to outdo the *Hawkbill* in our exercises.

One afternoon, making a submerged approach on my old boat, we managed to sneak in and surface within easy torpedo range, and I sent Worth a gleeful message: "BANG, YOU'RE DEAD." He came back with: "THAT'S ABOUT ENOUGH FROM THE JUNIOR BOAT." It was hard to realize that these child's games were only a brief interlude before the real thing. I had to keep reminding myself that there was no play ahead, that the depth charges would be in dead earnest when they came. Like Tolstoy's hero, I found myself thinking no one could really want to kill so fine a fellow as I.

The country we were passing was some of the most desolate and abandoned in the world, and Darwin itself, when we arrived, turned out to be an outpost surrounded on all sides by desert or jungle, still bearing the scars of a Japanese bombing attack early in the war. There was a little oil barge there, among the sunken ships that still filled the harbor, and with the other two subs we tied up alongside it for refueling and went ashore. Worth and Hank and I got together for a few beers. My head quartermaster and two of the motor machinist's mates went to visit the quartermaster's brother, who was stationed in Darwin, and when the time came for us to get under way, they had not returned.

I had always prided myself on punctuality, and to be delayed at the very beginning of my first patrol made me furious. I would have left them in Darwin, but they were good men, seasoned submariners, and irreplaceable. So we waited and fumed for twenty minutes before they showed up. They had run out of transportation, and the bus they thought would bring them back wasn't running. Still hot from the embarrassment of seeing the crew of my old boat, the *Hawkbill*, standing at the rail while we missed our sailing time, I gave them hell for the delay and promised they would be restricted to the boat when we got back to Perth. By the time we did get in from that patrol, of course, I had long since forgotten it, but that day in Darwin I took it as an evil omen. We were off on the wrong foot. Would things continue to go wrong?

We were on our way now, with no stops ahead. We

went through the Malay Barrier, the Macassar Strait, and the Sulu Sea, and out into the South China Sea, through a pass in the Philippines, to our patrol station. Insofar as the enemy was concerned, it was an uneventful journey, the tedium broken only by occasional planes, sailing vessels, and mirages. But the mirages could be very troublesome. The water in the Sulu Sea was as flat and calm as a pane of glass, and it produced some remarkable effects. A piece of driftwood floating in the water could sometimes be sighted twelve or fifteen miles away, and the lookout would swear it was a ship. The radar wouldn't pick it up, but the illusion was often so convincing that all we could do was grit our teeth and go toward it until it got below the horizon and we could identify it.

Three days out of Darwin we ran into real trouble of a mechanical nature. Our Torpedo Data Computer, without which our effectiveness in attack would be considerably limited, went out of commission. For nearly two days we worked on it, while my conviction grew that everything was going to go wrong on this patrol. At last it became obvious we couldn't fix it without some spare parts.

Not too hopefully, I sent a dispatch asking for help from any southbound sub. Perth responded almost at once, directing me to rendezvous about a hundred miles north of our position with my classmate, Fran Greenup of the *Hardhead*. So about one o'clock the next morning the *Flasher* and the *Hardhead* came alongside, Fran passed us the gear, and we were ready to go. We had got the replacements not five hours after asking for help, and two thousand miles from the nearest friendly port — better service, as I noted in my patrol report, than anyone could expect alongside the tender.

On station in the eastern part of the South China Sea, the three subs in our pack took positions about twenty miles apart, and the endless hours of slow patrolling and anxious waiting began. It was quiet at first, and again I found myself analyzing my spirit of aggressiveness. It fluctuated remarkably. One day I would be nervous as a cat and wholly lacking in self-confidence; the next, I would feel capable of licking the whole Japanese fleet. I resolved to sleep more regularly, eat less foolishly, and even to watch my reading. I was engrossed in *Lee's Lieutenants* at the time, along with lesser literary works, and it was easy to discover that Douglas Southall Freeman's great work was on the good side of the ledger. Reading about these courageous men of another war, consoling myself with the fact that they too could make mistakes and yet sometimes bring victory out of confusion, I found myself more confident. In a position of command, a man can gain great comfort from the realization that blunders are not the exception in wartime; that instead, most actions are built on a series of mistakes, unexpected factors, and unpredictable chances.

It was, in fact, an unpredictable chance that catapulted us into our first engagement — we got off course.

For several days, as we watched with increasing tension for a sight of the enemy, the skies had been overcast. Visibility had been so poor we had been unable to get a good fix. But the fourth of December dawned bright and clear. I went up on the bridge with Phil Glennon at morning twilight and saw him get a good star sight; then, when he dropped below to work on his fix, I went to the wardroom for coffee.

Phil came in a few minutes later, looking pleased.

"I've got a good fix this morning, Captain," he said. "We're about fifteen miles west of where we ought to be."

It was a big relief to know just where we were. A few miles can make a world of difference when you're operating in a pack.

"Fine," I said. "Plot it and let me know our course back to position."

Phil nodded and bent over the plotting sheet, and I was lifting my cup for another drink of coffee when the messenger came in and handed me a dispatch from the radio shack.

It was from Worth Scanland on the *Hawkbill*, and some instinct told me it was big news. This is it, I thought. After all the waiting, this is it. As I handed the coded message to Kiko Harrison I could feel the hair begin to stand up on the back of my neck.

Kiko broke out the little black box and began decoding. The first word was "CONTACT."

Worth had spotted a convoy, a big one. He gave its course and speed, and added a typical wisecrack: "YOU TAKE THE ESCORTS, WE'LL TAKE THE GRAVY." But as we checked the convoy's location with our own, Phil and I looked at each other and grinned in delight. Our position fifteen miles off station put us directly ahead of the convoy. With any luck, at least some of the gravy — the big ships — would be ours.

I slid off the wardroom seat and began running for the

conning tower, Phil behind me. As we ran I could feel the atmosphere of the boat changing. The men of the *Flasher* sensed that something was about to happen, and without an order being given they began ambling quietly to their battle stations.

Tom McCants had the deck. I called up the hatch to him, giving him the direction to turn the *Flasher* so we would point toward the convoy, and raised the periscope to full height.

And there it was. I could see the sticks of the Japanese ships almost immediately, headed toward us.

From his position on the bridge, Tom couldn't see them, so Phil called the news up the hatch as I stood in the quiet conning tower, feeling the rush of blood to my skin, knowing the test I had dreamed and wondered and worried about since my earliest days at the Naval Academy was upon me at last. My day of command in combat had arrived. What would I do with it?

I turned the *Flasher* after a moment and ran parallel with the convoy long enough to check its course and speed and give Phil a look. Worth had pegged it perfectly. Phil went below to send him word we had made contact and were attacking and I stood there awhile, feeling utterly alone as I watched the enemy masts in the periscope.

"Okay," I called at last. "Turn toward her."

"Aye, aye, sir," Tom answered from the bridge. "Left full rudder." We swung around 180 degrees.

"Take her down, Tom."

He hit the diving alarm and the three lookouts poured down the hatch as we started easing under. Tom followed, grabbing the hatch lanyard and slamming the hatch shut behind him, and the quartermaster reached up and turned the wheel to seal it tight.

Tom gave me a searching look as he came down the ladder. He had not seen the convoy, but he knew generally what was ahead, and I could read in his face the same question I saw in the other faces as we moved to battle stations: How will this fellow work out on his first attack?

Phil came back up to the conning tower, took the is-was off its hook and draped it around his neck, beginning almost instantly to set courses and speeds on it. Tom moved back to the port after corner and began throwing the switches to start the Torpedo Data Computer. As the *clang-clang-clang* of the battle-stations bell died away, the sound of the TDC motors ground through the conning tower.

Eddie Atkinson, our assistant torpedo officer, came up and gave me the same look Tom had given me as he walked back to stand by the TDC. I answered him with a blank stare, feeling my face set and stiff. Two quartermasters came up to assist in working the tracker and keeping the log; Kiko Harrison pulled his tall frame up the ladder and walked aft, standing by for Eddie and Tom as a sort of general utility man. Below in the control room, I heard Snap Coffin speaking quietly to one of the planesmen.

For just a moment, as we leveled off at periscope depth, I looked around me at these men I had known so briefly but so intimately. I felt that I knew all about them, who their families were, how many children they had, what their hopes and aspirations were, man by man, and as I thought of it I said to myself again, God, how lonely this is. Subconsciously, I was still looking for the man who would give the ultimate commands. But this time I was the man, and something in the faces about me brought home my responsibility in a final and terrifying way.

One of the quartermasters had picked up the bug with which the periscope was elevated and lowered. I flipped my thumbs, the scope slithered up, and I took a look.

The weather had grown worse. The sea was covered with rain squalls. I could not expect to see the targets, anyhow, because they were still several miles away and our height of eye was only a few inches above the level of the sea, but the rain squalls worried me. If they continued, we were in for trouble.

A faint *ping-ping* sounded from the sonar gear. As I listened, it grew louder. The enemy's search sonar was busy.

For a while at least, with the rain all about us, we would have to operate blind, taking our cues from the TDC, which was generating the range on the assumed course and speed of the targets that we had fed it after our last look before submerging. And, as we moved through the rain-swept seas, hearing the pings of the Japanese sonar increase in volume, I began to get a feeling of frustration. This would be a fouled-up attack. I didn't have enough to go on. Why did the first one have to be like this?

Still nothing but rain in the periscope. I abandoned it and walked the two steps back to look at the dials on the TDC and talk it over with Phil and Tom.

"Sound, what's the bearing?"

"One propeller, bearing zero one five relative, Captain."

"How does that check, Tom?"

"That's pretty good, Captain. He may have zigged to the left."

"Okay. Watch it."

It was all a sort of guessing game at best. We didn't know just what targets were up there; we couldn't keep them all spotted on the TDC anyway; and we couldn't tell from the sound whether we were listening to the main target or one of the others.

I went back for another try at the periscope. Rain again. Exasperated, I called down the hatch to Snap Coffin in the control room.

"Bring me up another three feet, Snap."

"Aye, aye, sir."

The periscope slid higher out of the water, but it was no use.

"Oh, hell. Take me back down." And the game of hide-and-seek — a one-sided game, we hoped — continued.

"Still can't see a thing. What's the bearing?"

"High-speed screws bearing zero one zero relative, sir."

"What's it sound like to you?"

"High speed, Captain — probably a destroyer."

"Damn! Where the hell is he? Why doesn't the rain stop?"

Tom McCants stirred beside the TDC. "Generated range twenty-five hundred yards, Captain."

We were getting close now, too close for comfort. Through the sonar gear we could hear the *swish-swish* of propellers, and the pinging had become deafening. They've got us, I thought; they know we're here and they're coming after us. Almost frantically I swept the periscope. Nothing but the heavy, impenetrable curtain of rain in all directions.

"If we don't pick him up soon, he's going to get by us."

No one answered. For a second, angered by the silence, I wanted to turn away from the periscope, grab Phil and thrust him against it, and say, "All right, *you* take a look. You think I'm not doing it right? You try!"

And then, so suddenly it was almost as though I had never expected it, there it was, a gray silhouette looming up out of the rain squall — a destroyer, all right, and very close.

"There he is! Bearing — mark!"

"Zero one five relative!" Phil's voice was electric.

"Range — mark!"

"Two one hundred."

"Set!" Tom's voice had the same excited quality as Phil's.

"It's a destroyer," I told them. "Angle on the bow thirty starboard."

"Set." And Tom cranked it into the TDC.

Everything, it occurred to me, was different now. The instant I had seen that gray shape through the haze, it had been like the first kickoff in a football game. The fears, the inhibitions, the uneasy feelings that had been holding me back vanished. Here was the target, here was what I'd been trained to do, and I was reacting to it almost automatically, just as everyone else was.

"Down scope. . . . Right full rudder!" No time now to think he would be on our backs if we missed him, no time to wonder where the rest of the convoy was. Nothing to do now but swing the ship so we could get a relatively straight torpedo run, and fire ahead of him.

"Aye, aye, rudder's coming hard right."

I watched the helmsman's back as he turned the helm, watched the rudder angle indicator, and noted the painfully slow way in which the *Flasher* swung right. We needed more speed in the swing.

"Starboard stop. Port ahead full."

The boat began to swing more rapidly, churning up noise that the target might be able to hear. But it was our best chance for a good shot.

I stepped back for a moment to watch the problem generate on the TDC, where one little dial represented the enemy ship and another showed the way the *Flasher* was turning, turning, trying to point ahead of it. We weren't swinging fast enough to complete it in time.

"All right," I said abruptly. "We're going to fire on the swing."

When you fire a large-angle shot and the range is off, you miss. All I could hope was that we had his range so exactly that, firing while the *Flasher* was still turning in the water, at least one of the fish would hit.

"Stand by for final bearing. . . . Up periscope."

"Target bearing zero two seven relative." As the quartermaster raised the periscope, Phil grabbed its handles from behind and set the line on the relative bearing. I slapped my eye to it, and there was the target.

"Stand by."

Eddie Atkinson's voice was husky in the sudden hush. "Ready One."

"Fire One!" I gave the order in a shout, releasing all the elation and fear and hope of one of the most important moments of my life.

"Fire Two. . . . Fire Three. . . . Fire Four." My voice had grown so guttural that it frightened me a little.

The moment the fourth torpedo was out, I took a swing around with the periscope and spotted trouble.

"Bearing — mark! There's an escort headed at us. . . . Bearing — mark! There's another one."

Crash!

The first torpedo had hit the destroyer, and even as I swung the scope to look, a feeling of exaltation like nothing I had ever experienced before swept over me. By heaven, I had paid my way as a skipper now, no matter what happened. If we never accomplished another thing, even if none of us ever saw another day, we had justified our training, the cost of our boat, and the sacrifice of our lives. A submarine for a destroyer — it was a swap worth making if you had to.

Crash!

The second torpedo hit as I found the destroyer on the scope. I could see its water line rise as it was literally lifted out of the water. The whole ship vibrated. I knew it was doomed.

I continued my periscope sweep. The rain had thinned by now, allowing a little better visibility, and as I strained to see, new waves of excitement suddenly pounded over me.

For just abaft our port quarter lay what looked like the biggest damned tanker in the world.

"Mark! There's a tanker!"

"Bearing two one seven."

"Set."

"Angle on the bow port thirty."

"Set."

"Give her a speed of twelve knots, Tom."

"Aye, aye, sir. It's set."

"Looks pretty far. I'd say about twenty-five hundred yards."

"That's about right, Captain."

"All set."

It had all happened in a flash. I pulled my eye briefly away from the periscope and gave Phil a searching look.

"You think we ought to shoot, Phil? It's a beauty, but it's a lousy setup."

It was lousy because, with two escorts boiling at us, there was no time for anything. Our swing right to fire at the destroyer had lined our stern up with the tanker, which made the idea of a shot inviting, but that single snapshot look at him had been insufficient to get an accurate setup. We would be firing by guesswork, and we would have to go deep in a hurry. Moreover, the tanker would almost certainly be turning after the attack he had just witnessed.

"Yes, let's try it, Captain."

"Okay. Stand by aft."

"Ready aft." I knew without looking that the palm of Eddie Atkinson's hand was poised over the firing key.

"Stand by. . . ." I put the periscope crosswise carefully on the midship section of the tanker.

"Fire Seven. *Bring me up, Snap!*"

Down in the control room, Snap had been wrestling frantically with the trim ever since we'd fired the four quick ones at the destroyer. With all the maneuvering, and now with a torpedo being fired aft, he had momentarily allowed the periscope to dip under.

"Aye, aye, sir. Got to have some speed."

"All ahead two thirds." The escorts were getting too close for me to wait for another look. "All right, fire a spread of four torpedoes."

"Aye, aye, sir."

The torpedo in Tube Eight went out on an automatically generated spread, and the periscope broke surface again.

"Check fire!" I called. "He's turning away." The tanker was ponderously changing course to his left. With a poor setup and only a guess as to his range and speed at the out-set, it would be foolish to waste any more torpedoes. "Bear-ing — mark! There's the escort almost on us. Flood nega-tive. Take her deep. Rig for depth charge."

The moment I passed the word, the helmsman automati-cally reached up and turned off the electric fan in the con-ning tower, and I thought again how ridiculous this bit of routine seemed — turning off a one-eighth-horsepower mo-tor so it wouldn't be heard by an escort. Down below, we could hear the clatter of levers as the planesmen shifted from power to hand on the bow and stern planes, and the sudden silencing of the air-conditioning motors. The motor generators that ran the lighting system quit their whine as the lights were shifted to battery. Even the power steering was abandoned as the helmsman quietly shifted to hand steering. The propellers were still at two-thirds speed as we dropped through the water, because the escorts had seen our periscope and for a while speed would be worth the cost of propeller noise.

And then, just as our morale was beginning to ebb while we waited for the first depth charge to explode, we heard through the hull of the boat a distant roar, and then, six seconds later, another.

"My God," Phil breathed. "We hit him!"

We looked at each other in amazement. By all the rules, those fish couldn't have hit, but clearly they had.

"You know what? We must have guessed wrong on his speed, and his turn slowed him down just enough to make up for it!"

I thought of some of the mistakes in the Civil War that had helped produce victories. "Phil," I said, "I'll tell you what it is. There are some days when a guy just can't do anything wrong."

The first depth-charge attack came then, with a jarring roar, and we slowed to one third. If we survived it, our job was now to be completely silent, to sneak away, to hope the sonar operators on the escorts would lose us.

We were sweating by now, as the heat of all the engines and motors began to seep through the boat. Tom McCants pulled off his shirt with extravagant care to be silent. A couple of others in the fire-control party followed suit. Through the hull we began to hear the increasing *chum-chum-chum* of the escort's propellers as he came nearer on his return trip.

"If he drops them now," Phil whispered, "they're going to be close."

Like an echo to his words, a splash sounded through the

sonar gear — the sound of the depth charges hitting the water. We waited miserably, visualizing the depth charges sinking toward us, set to go off at a depth we could only hope wasn't the same as ours.

It was not a long depth-charging, but it was very close indeed. Our depth was all that saved us; the escort thought we were higher in the water than we were, and set his charges accordingly. Shaken by it but filled with a tremendous exhilaration, we slipped away to the south and gradually the sound of the depth charges grew fainter.

Looking around in a moment of quiet reflection, I thought I could sense a change in the attitude of the men about me. We had been through an attack together now, and henceforth, for better or worse, there would never again be that wall of watchful waiting that had stood between us before. We were all on the same team.

"Better reload now."

Even when you can make noise, reloading the torpedo tubes is a back-breaking job. When you do it while the enemy is on top of you, it is excruciating. The big two-thousand-pound fish have to be snaked into their tubes with great care for quietness after the tubes have been pumped dry and the inner doors opened. But in their holiday mood, the men of the *Flasher* could do anything and do it well.

We had wiped out a destroyer and at least severely damaged a tanker, and there was reason to celebrate. But even as I exulted over it, I was aware of a faint sense of unease in the back of my mind. We would have to go back. There was the tanker to seek out and finish, if it was still afloat, and there were doubtless other ships we had not yet seen.

But another attack meant another depth-charging, and I dreaded it. We had been outrageously lucky already, lucky to hit the tanker, lucky to escape those depth bombs that had been dropped directly over us, and I hated like hell to press our luck.

But it had to be done. I told Snap to bring us back up from the depths, and while we were still rigged for silent running, I turned to Phil.

"Let's get the crew back at battle stations."

He passed the word through the boat, and as the men drifted to their stations, I turned back to the periscope and waited, the palms of my hands a little damp, for the word from Snap.

"Periscope depth."

"Okay, Snap. Up scope." The tube came up and, as I watched, the scope broke surface. I took a wide sweep.

"Damn. It's still raining. You can't see far. . . . Mark! We hit him, we hit him! Phil, take a look at this!"

Off in the distance, colossal billows of black smoke rose from the stricken tanker. We hadn't dreamed those explosions, then. We really had hit him. Phil looked and drew in his breath in delight.

"He's a dead one, Captain. He'll never move again." Idly he swung the periscope around. "Hold on, here's another destroyer!"

I pushed my face to the periscope. Sure enough, there was a destroyer, almost identical with the one we had sunk.

"Bearing — mark!"

"Zero two zero."

"Angle on the bow ninety starboard. Speed zero."

"Speed *zero?*" Tom McCants couldn't believe it. "What's he doing, Captain?"

"I don't know. He couldn't be the same destroyer we torpedoed. That guy would have a hole in his side."

"Well, why is he lying to?" Phil couldn't understand it either.

I tried to puzzle it out. He had a big searchlight and was sending out some kind of signals, and the sound of pinging was loud on our sonar equipment. Had we blundered into a trap?

"Beats me. He must be listening." The more I thought of it, the better I liked the idea. Suppose this was an inexperienced skipper, nervous over the damage we had done already, going wild in an effort to locate us. Wouldn't he maybe decide it was worth the risk of lying to in order to listen for us better? It would be a terribly foolish thing to do, but it was true he could hear us better with his own propellers halted.

But there wasn't time to debate his motives, for I knew at least one of the smaller escorts was nearby. Why not go in and have a try at the destroyer? If we could get in to firing range, it should be no trouble at all to put two torpedoes into him. Then we could put two more into the stricken tanker, which we didn't want to leave for the enemy to tow away.

"What do you think of this setup, Skipper?" Phil asked, his face worried.

"Let's not think. If that guy wants to sit there and let us shoot at him, it's our job to accommodate him."

He grinned. "Aye, aye, sir."

We began moving in, very gingerly and tenderly. If he really was up to something we hadn't guessed, it would pay to be on our guard.

"Bearing — mark. There's another escort on our port bow, coming this way. Down scope. . . . I don't think he saw us."

The rain had closed in again, making it so hard to see that my hopes rose. Surely nobody could pick out our periscope in this water. Still, I was disturbed by what I heard. Not only was the pinging of the enemy sonar loud in our ears, but the sound of screws was all around us.

I tried another look, and let out a yelp of alarm.

The destroyer's searchlight was directly on the *Flasher*'s periscope.

We had blundered into something, then. He had us spotted, and was pointing us out to one of the escorts. I started to signal for the quartermaster to lower the scope.

But before I could move my thumbs, something strange about that brilliant light forced me to take another look, and I let out a fervent sigh of relief.

It was blinking irregularly. He wasn't pointing us out to anybody; he was sending a message in code to someone beyond us, and our periscope just happened to be in the path. Though for a moment I could imagine that his message read "GOOD-BY, GEORGE," I realized he hadn't seen us at all.

"Let's get this over with," I breathed. "Down scope. Open the outer doors."

The telephone talker repeated the order, and I watched till the conning-tower indicators showed that all six outer doors on the forward torpedo tubes were open.

"All right, stand by for a final setup."

"Ready."

"Up scope. Bearing — mark!"

The target was still lying to, but he had drifted so that now he was almost in front of the tanker. Only the stern of the blazing tanker could be seen under the overhang of the destroyer's stern. And, moving in fast on our port bow, came the nearest escort.

"We're going to have to fire. We'll take the destroyer first, and then the tanker. Stand by."

"Ready."

I took careful aim at the forward half of the destroyer.

"Fire One." The boat shuddered, and I swung toward the target's afterpart.

"Fire Two." A swing back to the escort now; he was almost on top of us. Back again along the deck of the destroyer to his stern, to pick up the tanker in the background.

"Fire Three!" And then, with no change in bearing, because I could see no more of the tanker to aim at, "Fire Four! . . . Take her down!"

Air from the negative tank rushed into the boat with a roar, and we started down. The periscope was hardly under when the escort rushed over for his first attack.

Boom!

"That's the first one hitting the destroyer, Captain." Phil had his eye on the stop watch.

Boom!

"That's the second one. He's dead, Captain."

Boom!

Phil's eyebrows shot up. "My God, the third one hit the destroyer, too!"

I nodded. From the timing, it had to be the destroyer. I hadn't given quite enough of a lead to miss it.

Boom!

"Captain," said Phil in a tone of awe, "that destroyer must be mincemeat."

We had missed the tanker, but it would wait. Four torpedoes in a destroyer, when one is enough to do the job!

Down we went then for the depth-charging. This time it was not so bad and not so long. A few charges exploded close enough to shatter light bulbs and rock the boat, but the escorts clearly didn't have their hearts in it, with both destroyers gone from the convoy. As we slipped away to the southwest, the *Flasher*'s crew went wild with delight.

It was easy to give the order to come back to periscope depth this time. I swept the entire horizon with the scope. The destroyer was gone, disintegrated. The tanker was still stopped, and burning fiercely. The escorts, all that remained of the convoy whose sticks we had seen in the early morning, were far off in the distance.

My legs felt like old rubber, but my attitude had deteriorated from humility and exultation to downright cockiness. On our first attack, we had sunk two deadly enemy destroyers and grievously wounded a tanker. All that remained was to finish it off, and nothing could stop us from that.

There was nothing else to shoot at except the small escorts, which weren't worth the trouble, so we lurked low, reloading, resting and celebrating, until they went away.

When we came back to periscope depth for another look around, we saw the *Becuna*. It was our first contact with either of our sister subs since the message from the *Hawkbill* had launched the long day's attack. We surfaced, I exchanged blinker messages with Hank Sturr of the *Becuna*, and both subs proceeded cautiously toward the great billows of smoke that marked the dying tanker. We found her abandoned, so Hank went on his way and I sent a message to Captain Bryant, our wolfpack commander, that I was going to stay and sink her after dark.

In a couple of hours we were ready. Moving carefully again to assure that we weren't falling into a trap, we came almost alongside the tanker.

She was a desolate sight, this ten thousand-ton ship, very low in the water on an even keel, with every stick afire and black smoke still pouring up from her cargo of oil. We cruised around her several times without finding any sign of life.

Suddenly I had an idea, and turned to Jim Hamlin, our communications officer.

"Jim, I'm going to make a movie that will be the greatest production number of the war. Get the camera."

My plan was to set the camera grinding just before we put the torpedo into the tanker, and to hold it on the target during all the fireworks that would follow. Jim grinned, got the movie camera, and showed me how to use it. Waving it around with a great air of authority, I set up the camera angles.

We would fire a stern shot, I decided, in order to conserve our bow torpedoes, and we'd get in to about eight hundred yards and line everything up perfectly so the explosion would be smack in the center of the picture and the flames would shoot out in their most spectacular fashion.

At last all was set. I started the camera rolling.

"Stand by. . . . Fire!"

The camera ground away, the torpedo hit, and every man on the bridge of the *Flasher* whooped with glee at my failure as a film producer. For the torpedo, instead of touching off a holocaust, put out the fire altogether. The tanker sank in utter darkness.

But it didn't bother me for long. I drifted off to sleep that night, as we headed back toward our scouting line, with a feeling of gratitude and pride such as I had not experienced since the junior football team scored its first touchdown at prep school back in Memphis, with me carrying the ball. Only one thing was lacking. I wished Ann were with me.

12

Jackpot

ON THE FOLLOWING SUNDAY, the reading of the Bible in the wardroom became, by common consent, a fixed part of our weekly routine. An old joke and a sailor's reverence were responsible.

Our submarines did not carry chaplains. On some of the subs, the captains conducted regular religious services, but most skippers felt unqualified, as I did. If it had not been for a Negro steward's mate named Page, the *Flasher* would never have had a formal observance of the Sabbath.

It all began two Sundays before our attack on the convoy. Eddie Atkinson, our commissary officer, always suffered at our hands when the meals were not up to our expectations, and dinner on this particular evening was especially dull.

"Eddie," I said, "these meals are beginning to remind me of a verse in the Bible. It's Hebrews 13:8, I believe."

He didn't know whether to be pleased or not.

"What's that, Captain?"

"Oh, no," I said, "I'm not going to tell you. It'll do you good to look it up."

Eddie stuck his head out the door and spoke to Page. "Can you find me a Bible?"

"Yes, sir!"

He was back with it in a minute, and one glance at him made me feel thoroughly ashamed. Page was a devout man, and as he smiled at me it was clear what he was thinking: this was Sunday night, and the new captain of the *Flasher* had directed that the Bible be brought in for devotions.

"Thank you, Page. That will be all." I wanted to be sure he was gone before Eddie found and read the verse I had cited: "Jesus Christ the same yesterday, and today, and forever."

The next Sunday evening, after we had gathered in the wardroom for the evening meal, Page appeared. He had the Bible in his hands, and he offered it to Phil Glennon.

"I knew you'd want it, sir," he said.

Phil and I exchanged glances. There was but one thing to do, and we both knew it. I nodded slightly, and Phil thanked Page, opened the Bible to Psalms, and read a few verses to his startled fellow officers.

I forgot about it during the week that followed, but on the next Sunday, the first one after our attack, Page was back again.

"A lot to praise the Lord for this week, Captain," he said.

After he was gone, we talked it over and decided Page was right. We *did* have a lot to praise the Lord for. From then on, we never let a Sunday go by without reading the Scriptures, with all the reverent attention Page could wish.

After the attack on the convoy we moved into a new area, and as the days passed, it became increasingly obvious these waters were unfruitful. Except for a few planes and a Japanese hospital ship, which of course was out of bounds to us, we sighted nothing for days. Phil fretted more than the rest of us. He was counting heavily on the prospect of firing all our torpedoes in time to get back to Perth, and his sweetheart, by Christmas. So when he brought me our new orders on December 13, he was smiling hopefully. We were to leave the wolfpack and proceed to take station off the entrance to Manila Bay. Our forces had reason to believe some major ships were about to come out of the bay, and they wanted someone there to report it when it happened.

Any change was welcome, but I was dubious about this one. Manila Bay is a very large body of water, far too large for one small submarine to keep an eye on. If we entered it submerged, ships might well pass through the mouth of the bay without our seeing them. Not only that but it was hotly patrolled and the water was shallow in spots and believed to be mined. The thought of the *Flasher's* undertaking to carry out its assignment under such circumstances reminded me of the paper blockades I had read about in naval history, where nothing but an unsupported piece of paper or a token force was expected to keep ships in or out of a particular area.

But we had been directed to go, so we went. We ran at full speed all that night and arrived on station north of Lubang Island, southwest of the entrance to the bay, the next morning. Our forces were scheduled to make an air strike that morning, and we were eager to arrive in time for a look. None of us had ever seen an air strike, and I was especially interested because I was almost positive a cousin of mine, Fred Jacobs, would be in one of the planes.

As we approached the Philippines that morning, we saw an awesome sight. The air was filled with planes that we knew were our own. It seemed there were thousands of them, zooming over Manila and Subic Bay and dropping their bombs as the Japanese antiaircraft fire blossomed from the ground.

We crowded onto the bridge to watch. It was such a comforting thing to see our own forces in such strength, and obviously belting the enemy so thoroughly, that we lost all sense of our own vulnerability. By the time the air attack reached its height, we were within easy sight of the land forces around the bay.

"Look at that!" Phil yelled. "Did you see that explosion? We're really giving 'em hell!"

"Yeah," said Tom Burke. "Man, this is the way a war ought to be fought — surrounded by our own planes. It's wonderful."

It hadn't occurred to us that, because of gas limitations and other reasons, the planes would go away very soon and leave us naked before the enemy. The voice of the lookout brought our enthusiasm to a halt.

"Plane low and dead ahead . . . headed this way."

Phil turned. "My God, it's a Jap!"

And it was. He had his bomb bay open, and he was coming for us. So down we went, feeling somewhat shaken and realizing that although our planes made a beautiful display, they were not much help to the *Flasher* at the moment.

We still had to report to Admiral Christie that we had arrived on station. After a while, feeling a little rueful over our required presence in this Japanese hotbed to survey alone a port as big and important as Manila, we surfaced and sent a message that we were conducting our "paper blockade" as ordered. I doubt that the admiral was particularly amused.

We patrolled submerged the rest of the day and surfaced that night for a better look, but the Japanese planes gave us no peace. At first we joked about it, assuming the planes that chased us under came our way by chance. But it soon became something less than a joke. Every time we surfaced, something would come after us, and after a while it became nerve-wracking. Night was the time we counted on to charge our batteries, but the planes were making that impossible.

When we surfaced for the fourth or fifth time shortly after midnight and had to start running from a patrol boat the minute we got up, we quit laughing entirely. He came toward us out of the bay, and we decided to try to outrun him. But he was faster, and the range was closing steadily when the messenger brought me a new order from the admiral. We were to leave the area at once and proceed to another scouting line farther north.

No order was ever carried out more promptly. We made a radical change of course away from land and kept right on going. The escort didn't follow us into deep water.

By morning we were well away from Manila, and after two nights without sleep I fell into my bunk and slept until the middle of the afternoon.

Meanwhile, a terrific drama was going on somewhere in the China Sea. It involved my friend Johnny Hyde, skipper of the *Bergall*, and his boat.

We picked up a garbled message of his to Admiral Christie, reporting the *Bergall* had torpedoed a heavy cruiser, cutting it half in two, and had been hit in turn by a shell from a light cruiser escort. The shell had knocked off her forward torpedo-loading hatch and three square feet of hull.

That meant the *Bergall*, alone in enemy waters, was unable to dive. We waited anxiously around the radio shack to learn what the admiral would say.

His answer directed Johnny to head for a certain location and rendezvous with another submarine, which was to take off his crew and destroy the *Bergall* if necessary. It was the best answer that could be made, of course, but the future looked black for the *Bergall*. Her position must be known, at least in a general way, by the light cruiser that had hit her, and any plane or ship that came along could see her as she limped through the water incapable of diving.

It was days before the good news came through: the *Angler* had met her, right on schedule, taken off most of her crew, and begun escorting her back to Fremantle. That trip was surely one of the most remarkable of the war — two submarines, one of them a cripple, moving right down through the South China Sea, the Java Sea, past Singapore, and through the Barrier without ever being sighted. It gave us all new pride in the Submarine Service. The *Bergall* was repaired and back in service within a month.

We spent an unproductive day or two patrolling with the members of our old wolfpack and then were ordered away to still another assignment. Japanese warships had been reported in Camranh Bay, near Saigon on the coast of Indochina, and the *Flasher* and the *Becuna*, in company with the *Hoe*, the *Dace*, and the *Paddle*, were directed to take a look. The five of us moved to our new area, formed a scouting line at right angles to the coast, and began looking for game.

The water off Camranh Bay is not ideal for submarines. We were operating in depths of twenty to fifty fathoms, not nearly enough for comfort, for a submariner's greatest feeling of security comes from knowing that he can go deep when he is depth-charged. But if we could find targets, even in shallow water, it would be worth the risk.

We knew now we wouldn't make it back to Perth in time for Phil and his Dorothy to have a Christmas wedding, for we hadn't yet expended our torpedoes and our orders were to stay on patrol until December 26. On the twenty-first, after two days without enemy contacts, I asked permission to leave the convoy and move up off Hon Doi Island, a spot a little farther up the coast that struck me as better than the area we were in for intercepting convoys. Permission was granted, and we moved up.

I was at a low ebb — tired, eager to head back for Perth, and nervous about pushing into that shallow water. As we arrived on our new station, I just didn't feel like fighting a war. And while I was in this mood, opportunity knocked.

About nine in the morning, word came down that a patrol boat had been sighted. I went to the conning tower, where Tom Burke was on watch.

"There he is, Captain. Coming up from the south."

I looked through the scope. It was a small boat, a couple of miles away and headed in our direction.

It would have been a simple matter to go below periscope depth and let him pass over, trusting he would be unaware of our presence, but I didn't like the idea. We were in close to shore, in water not nearly deep enough for comfort, and in such a situation a patrol boat can be a deadly foe for a submarine. I told myself there would be no harm in moving out into deeper water until he got by, and then moving back in.

"Let's move out, Tom, and let him pass."

"Aye, aye, sir. . . . Take course zero nine zero."

The patrol boat was slow. It took an unreasonably long time for him to pass, and before we could move back in, it was too late.

I was in the wardroom when the messenger came down.

"Contact in the conning tower, Captain."

Tom's eye was on the scope as I came up the ladder. "Looks like a big convoy, Captain, pretty far inshore."

I looked, and ground my teeth. Four big, fat enemy tankers were headed up the beach in parade, with three escorts dancing in the rough waters along their starboard beams and a destroyer bringing up the rear. If we had been on their port side where we belonged, they would have made a magnificent target. But I had moved out of position to make way for a little patrol boat, and now it was too late to get back.

"Let's try to get them," I said automatically, knowing we couldn't.

We went down to ninety feet and began an approach as the fire-control party gathered and the *Flasher*'s men went to battle stations.

"Bring her up to periscope depth."

The bearing was changing to the northward. Speeding through heavy seas, they were getting past us.

"There's the destroyer. Take a look at him, Phil."

He looked. "Captain, we could probably hit the destroyer."

"Right. But the chances are poor at this range and in this rough water. And if we do shoot, there'll be no chance of getting the convoy." But a darned good chance, I added to myself, of getting a whale of a depth-charging.

Phil nodded. "To hell with the destroyer if we can get the convoy, sir."

We made another long, grinding effort to get it, but it was hopeless. I stood at the periscope, cursing myself, my lack of aggressiveness, and my bad judgment, as the stark realization mounted that the choicest target I would probably ever see had passed me because I had given in to a momentary weakness.

Gradually I became aware of something else. For the rest of my life I would hate myself as a coward unless I surfaced, made an end-around, and redeemed myself. And when I considered it in that light, the decision wasn't too difficult. I didn't like the prospect of surfacing in those rough and heavily patrolled waters, but the alternative was even worse.

I waited a few minutes after the last of the big tankers disappeared over the horizon.

"Secure from battle stations. . . . Secure the fire-control party. . . . Stand by to surface."

"Aye, aye, sir."

"Get ready on four main engines. We're going to plow into this sea with everything we've got."

The order passed aft, and the answer came back from the maneuvering room. "Ready on four main engines."

"Very well. Surface."

The surfacing signal sounded and the ship lurched to the surface, immediately beginning a heavy roll in the bucking sea. The lookouts, the officer of the deck, and I clambered up to the dripping bridge.

"Open the main induction. . . . All ahead full."

As the boat picked up speed, the bow began to dip and rise in the heavy seas coming down from the north. The desolation of the scene fitted my mood. I felt I was at the very nadir of my career. I called myself every name in the book. I was a failure, and a coward as well; I should never have been accepted in the Navy at all; the idea that anyone should have entrusted me with command was incredible.

An end-around depends on speed. The idea is to surface out of sight of the enemy, work up all the speed you can get, steer courses that will keep the tops of your targets' masts in sight without revealing your own presence, and finally

get around in front where you can wait for them. Foul
weather or not, we would have to move fast.

Rough-water procedure was indicated, for every time the
Flasher dipped, water poured over the bridge. Instead of
putting the lookouts up in the periscope shears I kept them
on the level with the officer of the deck, where they could
hold on to something solid. One of them was detailed to
stay with his hand on the hatch. Whenever the officer of the
deck saw a rough sea coming, he yelled, "Shut the hatch!"
The hatch banged shut, the sea boiled over the bridge, im-
mersing all of us, and as it drained away, the lookout opened
the hatch.

But a submarine going into a heavy sea doesn't make
much speed at best, and the Japanese convoy was a fast one.
It looked hopeless. I continued to stand there, drinking salt
water, fighting the wind, expecting to be chased under by a
plane at any instant, and still cursing myself in all the lurid
terms that occurred to me. Already, in the back of my
mind, I was trying to think of some mellifluous phrase for
the patrol report, to explain why the convoy got away.

After a couple of hours the weather began to change.
The seas abated, the wind died down, and we began to
make better speed. But against this advantage was the increasingly painful fact that we had lost the masts of the
convoy. According to the few checks we had got on its
speed while we were submerged, we should have picked
them up on the high periscope in about three hours, or even
sooner. But although we raced along all afternoon at maximum speed, looking and hoping, we never caught sight of
them. The probability that they had ducked into one of the

little bays along the coast and lost themselves to us entirely grew stronger with each fruitless hour.

As the afternoon wore away, I went bitterly to the wardroom for a glum dinner at which no one spoke to me and I spoke to no one. I could imagine they were thinking the same things about me that I had thought on occasions in the past when a superior officer had seemed to fail in courage or aggressiveness. After dinner, I divided my time between trying to read and making frequent trips to the bridge. Each time the empty seas, now calm as glass, reproached me.

By now we were far out of our assigned area and in that of some other submarine. This was permissible in a case of hot pursuit, but it was not to be overdone. I decided to break off the chase if we had sighted nothing by one o'clock the next morning.

About midnight I paid another trip to the conning tower, where Phil was busily plotting our track against what he could see of the landmarks along the coast.

"Any sign of them?"

"No, sir, not yet. I'm afraid they must have holed up for the night."

We looked at each other hopelessly in the darkness of the conning tower. "Well, let's give it another hour, and then we'll go back to station."

"Yes, sir." Phil's shoulders sagged and he turned back to his plotting chart.

One o'clock came with no report from the bridge. We had all become convinced we were burning up fuel at full speed for no purpose. I hoisted myself into the conning tower to tell Phil to give up the chase and found myself listening halfheartedly to an argument he was having with the quartermaster.

"No, it couldn't be," Phil was saying as I came up the ladder. "That's Tortue Island."

"But, sir, I've been watching it for five minutes, and the bearing hasn't changed."

Phil leaned over the radarscope with renewed interest. "What's that? What's the bearing now?"

"It's three three six true, sir. It's been that for at least three minutes."

"By God, you may be right."

Suddenly hopeful, I stuck my face between theirs, and the three of us stood for several minutes watching a vague little point of luminescence on the radar screen and comparing it with the bearing of the gyro repeater around it.

"Bearing still three three six, sir."

"You're right!" Phil's voice was a triumphant shout. "That's not Tortue, that's something under way! That's the convoy, Captain!"

The relief that swept over me was tremendous. I felt like a prisoner who has been reprieved on his way to the death chamber. This time, I told myself exultantly, I was going to damage that convoy or die trying. This time no one could say or even think that Grider's hesitation had lost the opportunity for us.

"Pass the word for the tracking party to man their stations."

"Aye, aye, sir." A few hurried calls on the telephone

brought the *Flasher*'s officers to the conning tower. Pencils were broken out, the TDC was put into operation, and we began the first preliminary maneuvers in the deadly task of tracking the enemy target.

It soon became clear beyond doubt that this was indeed our escaped target of the morning before — a convoy of four great, beautiful, and unusually speedy tankers, with several escorts. By now I was on the bridge, boring through the darkness with our best binoculars and gradually picking out blobs that resolved themselves into ships. Phil, closely studying the radar in the conning tower, was sending up every scrap of information he could get.

"They're mighty close to the coast, Captain. Too close for comfort."

"How many escorts, Phil?"

"Can't be sure, Captain. At least one destroyer, and some smaller ones. The destroyer acts like he's got radar."

The tedious job continued. We must pull up abreast and get into a position on the starboard bow from which we could penetrate the screen of escorts and work in for an attack. When we were seven miles off the starboard bow of the leading tanker, we slowed our engines and turned carefully toward.

"Where's the destroyer, Phil?"

"About abeam of the third tanker, Captain. If he stays there, we can get by."

"Okay, let's start in. All ahead standard. Call the ship to battle stations." The last was an unnecessary order. By now everyone, sensing the opportunity, had long since walked to his position, put on phones, picked up tools, done whatever was required to be ready when the *Flasher* met the challenge.

"Captain, the destroyer is moving up."

"Okay, Phil. I can see him now. He's abreast of the second ship. . . . Looks like he's going ahead pretty fast. . . . Turning toward us a little. . . . All stop." Judging from the destroyer's actions, it would have been foolish to push in, for it appeared that he either knew we were there or strongly suspected it.

"Right full rudder." We swung to a slightly divergent course from that of the convoy and opened out a little, carefully watching the destroyer, which instead of continuing in our direction stayed abeam of the leading target. His every move indicated he knew something was out there that threatened his precious convoy.

"Phil, we'll drop back and try coming in on the starboard quarter."

"Okay, Captain. Sounds like a good deal."

The propellers stopped and we lay in the water, letting the convoy pull by until we were abeam of the fourth ship.

"All ahead standard." It took fourteen knots to keep abreast of this speedy convoy. "Come left to course three hundred. Phil, keep an eye on that destroyer."

The starboard lookout sang out a warning from overhead: "Captain, the destroyer is dropping aft." I put the binoculars to my eyes and saw he had turned toward us and seemed to be putting himself between us and the convoy. He was patrolling that starboard side like a sheep dog.

"It may be just a routine maneuver. Let's keep going in."

"Range to destroyer five thousand yards, bearing steady." The word drifted up from the radar operator in the conning tower. "Range to destroyer four seven five zero, bearing steady."

I took another look. It was apparent the destroyer had sensed our presence once again and was interposing himself.

"The hell with this, Phil. Let's go up again and try it on the bow, and this time we'll go in no matter what he does."

"Aye, aye, Captain." There was a hint of doubt in Phil's voice. If the destroyer did know where we were, we'd never get by him. But if we torpedoed him first, the other escorts would be on us immediately and the convoy would probably get away.

The long, slow job of getting ahead of the convoy, with an advantage in speed of only four knots, was repeated. And when we were in position off the starboard bow again, the same situation arose as before.

"Captain, the destroyer's headed toward us. Bearing steady, range decreasing."

I took another long look at him through the binoculars. Should we risk an attack on the leading tanker, assuming only chance had brought the destroyer toward us again, or should we try again from another quarter? But we had tried that without luck. With the convoy hugging the shore line, we were blocked all along its port side. And I was grimly determined that, come what may, we were going to get in and get an attack on that convoy. There was only one other course of action.

"All ahead flank. . . . What's the convoy's course, Phil?"

"Convoy course zero zero eight, Captain."

"Okay, come to course zero zero eight. Phil, we're going to get ahead of the convoy, work in to the land side, and wait for them."

"The water's mighty shallow up there, Captain."

"To hell with it. I don't think the destroyer will follow us across. He must be using his radar, and those Japanese radars always fail when there's land behind the target."

"Okay, sir. We'll try." Phil was skeptical.

Now that we had settled on a positive plan, an electric excitement swept the bridge and the conning tower. I could feel it, and it felt good. We cut through the still water, four, five, eight, and at last ten miles ahead of the convoy. Then, safely out of danger of being sighted as we crossed ahead, we made the move.

"Left standard rudder."

"Rudder left standard, sir."

"Come left to course three two five."

The boat swung and steadied on the new course, presenting a small silhouette to the onrushing convoy but well ahead of it.

"What's the destroyer doing, Phil?"

"He's up close ahead of the convoy now, Captain. Looks like he's crossing over with us."

My heart sank. Even if he did cross over, we were still going to attack, but we would be at a terrible disadvantage, boxed in against the beach with little depth for diving and little room for maneuvering.

"Watch him close, Phil. We're going to attack no matter what the bastard does."

"Aye, aye, sir." Phil and every man aboard were with me now, determined, no matter what it took, to get the luscious convoy we had been pursuing so long.

We moved in close to the beach and turned toward the convoy.

"Secure the engines." The word was passed aft and the muffled roar of the engines abruptly halted.

"Shift to batteries."

"Aye, aye, sir. Ready to answer bells on batteries." The response came back from the talker in the maneuvering room.

And then we waited, the sinister land to our backs, the shallow water under our keel, the convoy ahead of us with the destroyer still in the lead, still apparently undecided whether to cross over or get back on the seaward side.

A small island lay a mile or so up the coast, and a lighthouse stood on the point of land opposite. Our charts showed a passageway for shipping between cape and island, although the lighthouse had been dark as long as we had been within sight of it. A quarter-moon was in the sky, obscured by a long cloudbank. We lay in a stillness broken only by the quiet hum of the radar mast as it turned, and tried to penetrate the blackness of that dark night with our eyes.

And now, as I forced my eyes closer against the binoculars and looked, not directly at the horizon but a little above it, I could see our prey approaching.

"Phil, I've got them in sight on the bridge. Jim, get on the TBT."

Jim Hamlin, on the bridge with me, dropped his binoculars and screwed his eyes against the massive binoculars of the Target Bearing Transmitter, which would transmit the bearing upon which it was trained — and by that, the bearing of the target — down to the fire-control party in the conning tower.

He spoke after a long minute. "I've got them, Captain. I've got the first big ship. Don't see the escort."

"Okay, Jim. Phil, have you got the destroyer on radar?"

"Yes, sir. He's still ahead. He may come this way."

At that instant, to our horror, the light in the lighthouse went on. It was off our port beam, so we were not silhouetted by it, but even so it was an unnerving sight. The enemy was all about us in the darkness, on land as well as sea. And did the light mean that the waters around the cape, the very waters where we lay, were mined? Was it to guide the convoy through mines we might blunder into at any minute?

The destroyer itself came dimly into sight now, a small blob just ahead of the heavy mass of the first tanker.

"Phil, what's he doing?"

"He's still there, Captain. No, wait. He's turning."

I held my breath. Which way would he turn?

"Range six two three five to the destroyer," I heard the radar operator report. "Range six two four seven to the destroyer. . . . Range six two seven five."

I exhaled gratefully. He was moving back to the starboard flank of the convoy. He was not crossing over.

By now, Jim Hamlin was giving a steady stream of bearings to the fire-control party. The convoy had stopped its zigzag plan as it approached the pass between the island and the lighthouse, and as the time for action drew near, the setup was beautiful, almost classical: a night surface attack, no escorts on our side, the targets not zigzagging, and, because of the long period of pursuit, an absolutely perfect solution to the target course and speed. There was nothing to do now but wait and hope that nothing would disturb the deadly serenity of the situation.

"Open the outer doors." I whispered the order, unable to shake off the feeling that because we could see the targets so clearly ahead of us, they must certainly see us, even though our needle bow was pointed directly at them and the silhouette we offered was blanketed by the land behind us.

"Phil, we'll fire three at the leading ship. . . . Then Jim will swing to the second one and we'll fire our other three bow shots at him. . . . Then we'll swing to the right and fire our four stern shots at the third one." It meant disregarding the fourth target, but these were such large tankers that at least three fish were required for each to assure success.

"Aye, aye, sir." Phil's voice was growing exultant.

The setting moon emerged gradually from the bank of clouds that had obscured it. It was directly behind us, so that at this final moment we were silhouetted to the ships in the convoy by its faint light. But the thought we might be seen hardly bothered me by now. My weariness of body and emotion left room for nothing but the conviction that we were committed and would attack now whatever happened — that and a feeling that destiny was on our side, or we would never have got this far.

The massive ships pressed onward, seeming almost to hang over us. When the range was down to fifteen hundred yards, I spoke to Jim.

"Stay on the midships section of the leading target. We're ready to shoot." Then, to Phil: "Okay. Fire when ready."

Phil and the fire-control party would time the shots, put the spread on them, and do all that remained to be done. I waited, feeling strangely at peace, for what would come.

"Fire One." Phil's voice came faintly up the hatch. "Fire Two. . . . Fire Three."

Jim Hamlin swung the TBT to the second ship.

"Mark . . . on target."

"Okay, Phil, stand by . . . stand by . . . all right, you can start firing."

"Fire Four. . . . Fire Five. . . . Fire Six."

While he was still giving the orders, we heard a hit on the first ship and saw a muffled light as the torpedo exploded.

The time for silence was over.

"All ahead full!" We bent on all the power we could.

"Right full rudder!" The stern of the *Flasher* began to swing around. We had almost completed the swing when we heard a click. . . . *Boom!* And the second tanker caught fire with a terrific explosion.

I gasped. I have never in my life seen a fire like that one: a ten-thousand-ton tanker loaded with oil, catching fire even as the oil was blown into the air by the torpedo. Almost in the same instant, the first tanker also burst into flames.

In the brilliant surge of light we stood out like actors on a stage. The escorts, the trees on the beach, the very rivets on the targets were like floodlit props about us. And there in the center of the stage was the *Flasher*, its deck bathed in light so brilliant it was almost blinding. Jim Hamlin, like a sensible man, grabbed his binoculars and headed for the hatch, assuming we were going to get out of there in a hurry.

But I was in the midst of a triumph more personal than any I had ever experienced in combat before. Whatever happened, nobody could say I was a coward. I had cleared myself of the burden of guilt that had ridden my shoulders all day, and at that moment I didn't give a damn whether the *Flasher* was sunk or not. I grabbed Jim as he headed for the hatch, just as Mush Morton had once grabbed me, and pulled him back. And in that blinding glare we took careful aim, fired four torpedoes at the third tanker, and then started our engines almost nonchalantly and headed south.

We had no sooner got started than the third tanker exploded. As the flames of the three burning ships blended across the water, the fourth tanker, untouched but frantically backing its engines, coasted up almost against the third. Whether he backed safely out, we never knew.

A mile away the escorts sat on the water like toys on the red-lit stage. The destroyer, which had gradually worked its way back down the starboard side of the convoy until it was almost abeam of the fourth tanker at the time of the attack, stood two miles away, off our port bow and almost abeam.

Now it swung around and, like us, headed south. The action produced an instant conflict of interests between Phil and me.

"Phil, this destroyer is awfully close. He's manning his forward gun now."

"Yes, sir, Captain. Can we come left? We're in awfully shallow water."

"Good Lord, no, Phil, we can't come left. We've got to get away from this destroyer."

"Yes, sir, but we can't run aground."

"I don't care, we can't turn toward that damned destroyer. He's got the gun unlimbered now. I can see the men on it without even using my binoculars. Can't we come right just a little?"

"No, sir, Captain, not a bit. This water's too shallow. We've got to come left."

As we moved down that alien coast, the whole scene assumed an uncanny quality, more like a dream than reality. It was as if the destroyer were keeping station on us — never coming any closer, never moving ahead or falling behind, sliding through the red waters in some eerie maneuver beyond understanding. I had no doubt he saw us, and every moment I expected him to turn toward us or let go with a broadside.

I sent the lookouts below and stood with my hand on the diving alarm, ready to submerge even in that shallow water if he turned toward us.

But the weird experience continued, and our silent companion made no move to close. We cruised south together at about eighteen knots for two full miles, while Phil begged constantly for permission to turn left and I insisted we would be lucky if we didn't have to come right.

Then, incredibly, the destroyer turned — not toward us, but away. He put on left rudder, swung around, and returned to the burning convoy.

I was never able to explain his actions. Perhaps his return was in answer to an appeal from the fourth tanker, but why he had not already turned toward us, why he never fired a shot, I have never understood. Perhaps he never saw us at all, though that seems almost impossible. Perhaps he thought there was another submarine in the vicinity of the convoy, and turned back to seek it.

Whatever the reason, he turned away, and our feeling of relief was indescribable. At last we could get away from that menacing shore.

"Okay, Phil. He's turned left. I'll give you five degrees."

And then, as he drew still farther away and we became convinced that he was really gone for good, we headed out for sea, out toward where the water was sweetly deep beneath us. The men came up from below, a few at a time, to see the show behind us. Even at a distance of four miles it was a memorable sight — an inferno of fire against a romantic tropical shore.

It was almost sensuously delightful now to feel the swelling fathoms beneath us. We stayed on the surface long enough to put in a moderate battery charge, and at daylight, after sending the admiral a message that I hoped did justice to the night's adventure, I told Snap to take us down to two hundred feet and head for Perth. On the entire *Flasher* there must have been no more than four or five men still awake. We gathered in the wardroom and relived the attack for a while before we turned in.

I didn't get up until four o'clock that afternoon, December 22. That night we had a message from Admiral Christie:

"WONDERFUL CHRISTMAS PRESENT GRIDER. CONGRATULA-
TIONS TO YOU ALL. COME ON HOME. REUBEN IS GOING TO BE
PROUD OF HIS OLD SHIP."

We wouldn't know it until the figures were all in after
the war, but the *Flasher* had just sunk more tanker tonnage
on a single patrol than any other submarine in the Pacific.

13

Mop-up

WE CROSSED THE EQUATOR west of Borneo on Christmas Day and celebrated by firing at floating mines. Awakened for the occasion, I mused sleepily on the strange fact that the sinking of six Japanese ships was responsible for the general air of joy and goodwill, even peace, on the *Flasher*. In the afternoon Phil organized a party. All hands gathered in the after battery to sing Christmas carols, and Phil himself played Santa Claus, delivering appropriate presents all around. The fattest man on board got a corset, the biggest eater was handed a small trough, Mac McCants got a wig to cover his baldness, and Tom Burke got a two-foot pair of shoes. I was given a baseball cap with a foot-long visor, amid snickers from the crew, who considered my constant use of a baseball cap a mild eccentricity. That night the *Flasher* quartet gathered around the microphone of the general announcing system, flashlights and songbooks in hand, and sang carols. For a moment I felt I had recaptured something of the spirit of Christmas, but even my solemn consideration of paradoxes earlier in the day could not erase an unchristian pride in our recent triumphs. A detached part of my mind reminded me that I had needed humbling on occasions in the past, and that something had always come along to accomplish it.

It came this time with the problem, physical and psychological, of getting past the Malay Barrier.

From the coast of Indochina we had proceeded downward through the South China Sea toward the Java Sea. There lay the Barrier, a chain of islands running out eastward from the Malay Peninsula, between us and the relatively safe waters of the Indian Ocean. We were returning a different way from the way we had come, and the key to the problem lay in Lombok Strait.

The strait separated the islands of Bali and Lombok, both in enemy hands. I had been through it only once, on the *Hawkbill*. That time we had made it without incident, but reports of submarine difficulties in the strait were numerous, and a brooding conviction grew in me that we would pay at Lombok for the ease with which we had escaped from our big attack.

We traversed Karimata Strait off Borneo on Christmas night and moved into the Java Sea. Two days later, nearing Lombok, I decided on a shortcut to the west of a little group known as the Kangeans. It saved us about a hundred miles and took us within easy sight of a small tropical island called Goa Goa, shimmering in the sunlight with sailboats clustered about it.

Superstitions develop easily in combat. I remembered we

had passed a carton of cigarettes to the crew of a sailboat as we began the patrol, and it — or something — had brought us luck. Why not try it for luck on the return? So we overtook one of the sailboats off Goa Goa and passed over some cigarettes and a few loaves of bread. The first loaf missed the boat and one of the natives jumped overboard after it, his teeth flashing in a big grin as he dived, and I waved at him and turned my eyes resolutely in the direction of Lombok Strait.

For all my inner forebodings, I felt cocky. When we sighted a plane headed toward the strait from Surabaja in midafternoon, I waited until the last minute before easing down to periscope depth. The minute he was out of sight, we were back on the surface and headed for the strait, too impatient to wait for dark.

Lombok Strait is about ten or twelve miles across, and in peacetime I am sure it looks gigantic. But the only touch of claustrophobia I had during the war came as we headed into it. It seemed painfully narrow as I thought of the shore battery on Bali. But we moved on in, and just about sunset the radar operator reported a contact at five miles, a little abaft our starboard beam. We looked and saw a patrol boat headed at us.

I didn't want to be forced under at all, least of all in Lombok Strait, so I turned away and bent on four engines in an effort to outrun him. He closed the range steadily for a while, until he was in to about three thousand yards, but still I wouldn't dive. I was bound and determined to go through the strait that night, knowing that if we delayed it now, the second try would be doubly hard.

He could have headed us off if he had altered his course to get between us and the strait, but he kept following us directly, and at last we worked up our speed until we began to pull away, at a rate of about a foot a minute. We made our last change of course and headed down the middle of the strait with the patrol boat dead astern as night fell. Then he opened fire on us.

At first, I refused to admit it.

"He's shooting, Captain," Tom Burke, the officer of the deck, told me with a note of urgency in his voice.

I shook my head hopefully. "No," I said, "he's signaling."

It was wishful thinking, and a minute later I had to admit it. He had what appeared to be a 20-millimeter gun on his bow, and the shells began falling all around us, astern, ahead, and on both sides.

Still I refused to dive. There were plenty of other escort vessels in the strait, and once we slowed down, there would be the devil to pay. The best course, I decided, was to take our chances with this fellow and keep running for the Indian Ocean. I sent Tom and the lookouts below and remained on the bridge alone.

And up there in the darkness I got my long-delayed humbling. No one on the *Flasher* ever knew what happened to me in those next few minutes.

We had worked out a plan in advance for a situation like this, and down in the conning tower they thought I was putting it into effect. It was a good enough plan: we had prepared a can filled with gunpowder and oil-soaked rags, with a fuse in it, and the idea was to light it in case of an attack by a patrol boat and throw it far overboard. It would explode and flare up, and the enemy would think it was us and chase it while we went merrily on our way.

The can was on the bridge beside me, but as the shells fell closer and closer to the *Flasher* I lost all enthusiasm for lighting even a match on the bridge. It would give them too good a point of aim. Instead, I dropped the can overboard and began trying to decide which portion of my anatomy I least wanted to be hit.

There were some pressureproof storage tanks on the bridge for storing our automatic weapons. They were circular, about eighteen inches in diameter, and good to hide behind except for one disadvantage. I found I could get only about one third of myself behind a tank at a time.

Too little has been written about the problem of what to expose if you have to expose something. It can be an agonizing one.

At first I crouched with my head and shoulders behind the tank, thinking to guard my upper extremities. A shot whistled past, my rear end twitched, and a horrible thought occurred to me.

"Good Lord!" I muttered. "If I get shot in the can, it'll be awful! What will I *say?*"

I turned nervously around, assumed a squat, and left my head exposed.

But of what value is an unimpeached buttocks if the head be missing?

I considered this question with increasing unease, and finally took a desperate step which I have never before confessed to anyone: when the firing was the thickest, there was a period when the U.S.S. *Flasher,* that gloriously triumphant weapon of Uncle Sam's Navy, was headed south through Lombok Strait at nineteen knots with no one on the bridge but the skipper, and no part of the skipper showing but the top of his head. I had solved the problem by retreating part way down the hatch.

So I was chastened for a while, until the patrol boat fell safely astern and I resumed my post with a fresh sense of humility and called Tom Burke to say it was safe now for him to come up. He came, and we were rejoicing together when we looked ahead and saw a second patrol boat coming up at us from the south.

This time there was indeed nothing to do but go under, so down we went, and I told myself that now we must endure the depth-charging we had earned, but hadn't got, on the twenty-second of December.

He passed directly over us, continued along his way, and never dropped a charge. Apparently he had never seen us. And, to make matters even better, when we went under, we shook the first patrol boat completely. Within an hour we were back on the surface, charging south and full of glee.

There was still the battery on Bali, at the south end of the strait, to get past. By now my cockiness was gone. As we got nearer, I grew tenser. We pulled over as close as we could to Lombok and eased along, holding our breath, and just at the moment I thought would be ideal for them to open fire, there was a flash of lightning in the sky over Bali and I almost jumped overboard.

It was fate's final lesson of the evening to me, that I could be cowed by a flash of lightning.

The battery never fired, and in a few minutes the *Flasher* began to pitch and dip, as it entered the long, glorious, wonderfully safe swells of the Indian Ocean.

Now we could relax and have some fun with Snap Coffin. Snap was the engineer, a social butterfly ashore but a very serious and earnest officer on shipboard. In observance of the custom that had seen me navigating the *Wahoo* home from her third patrol, Snap was given the job of navigator the rest of the way.

We were getting dangerously low on fuel, a fact he knew very well as engineer. This called for precise navigating, and Snap had had very little experience. He worried painfully for a day or so until his self-confidence began to return, and then the officers and crew of the *Flasher* teamed up against him and almost broke his spirit.

We were a good six hundred miles from the nearest land, heading for Exmouth Gulf on the northwest point of Australia, where we were to refuel. One day we were sitting in the wardroom when Snap came in to make his noon report to me.

He gave me our position, and I thanked him and asked if he was sure he was right.

"Yes, sir, I'm certain," he said. "That's our exact position. I got a fine fix this morning, and I've got a morning sun line and now a noon fix. I know exactly where we are." It was almost heartbreaking, in view of what lay ahead, to note his confident pride.

"Fine, Snap. How are we doing on fuel?"

"Well, we're going to make it. We'll just barely make it to Exmouth Gulf."

And then, with perfect timing, the messenger came in.

"Sir, the officer of the deck reports they have sighted land through the periscope."

I looked at Snap and silently invited an answer.

"No, sir!" he said heatedly. "It couldn't be land!"

"Maybe it's a mirage," I said easily. "Let's go take a look."

I got up and started slowly for the conning tower. Snap was dying to get there first, but he had to let me go ahead of him. In the control room I went up the hatch first and headed for the periscope. We were on the surface, but the periscope gave us a point of view far above that from the bridge.

As we came up the ladder we could hear the quartermaster saying, "Stand by . . . mark . . ." and singing out a bearing. The other quartermaster was busily writing it all down.

"Let me look," I said, and stood at the periscope for about a minute.

"By golly, you're right," I said at last. "That's land. Phil, look at this."

The exec moved over to the periscope.

"Let me look," Snap said, a note of rising concern in his voice.

"No, wait a minute, Snap," said Phil. "Captain, this is amazing. That looks like some kind of building on the shore line. Look there!"

So I looked, and agreed, and then reported that houses were coming into view, and passed the scope back to Phil, who saw the houses and other details. Snap's frantic pleas for a look were growing pathetic.

"Snap," Phil asked sternly, "where can this *be?*"

"It *can't* be," he yelled, but it was only a prayer. "It's a mirage!"

"Well," I said, "until we find out where we are, we'd better slow down. Snap, don't you think we'd better get a sounding?"

"*Warm up the fathometer!*" Snap howled tragically. "Take a sounding!"

The voice from the control room was the voice of doom. "Three fathoms."

"Captain!" a lookout called from the bridge. "We can see land from *up here* now!"

Poor Snap swarmed up the hatch, took a look around the vast seascape, and collapsed. Only the iron discipline of the Navy must have prevented him from killing somebody with his bare hands.

We almost used our one remaining torpedo a few miles out of Exmouth Gulf.

Radar reported contact on a ship that had not been reported to us. A bright moon was just rising, but all we could see was a smear on the horizon. We began to track it, and sent a message to Perth asking if there were any friendly ships in the area. A prompt negative came back.

Finally we maneuvered into position where the ship would pass between us and the moon. It was a submarine. Perth would have known beyond doubt if any of our subs were in the area. I considered firing on it, but decided to investigate further, so I made a swing around and got up ahead of it again to let it pass between us and the

MOP-UP   249

moon. This time we were closer. It looked like a British
sub.

I got out our little recognition-signal lamp, ordered the
torpedo-tube door opened, and had him cranked in on the
TDC, so we were ready to fire at command. Then I sent
him a recognition signal.

Nothing happened. I knew I would be justified in firing,
but somehow I couldn't bring myself to do it. I made another run around, got into firing position again, and this
time broke out a portable searchlight with a beam that
could be seen at night for miles. Again, no answer.

Once more we made the swing. This time we used our
eight-inch searchlight to challenge him. And this time we
could see clearly that it was a British submarine. We could
see no one on the bridge. He moved on with complete
nonchalance, neither answering nor diving nor changing
his course. To this day, that skipper doesn't dream how
close he came to being torpedoed.

We refueled at Exmouth Gulf, and a few days later were
back in Perth, where the first order of business was Phil
Glennon's wedding.

His bride was a beautiful girl from a fine family in Perth.
He had met her during a rest period two or three patrols
before, when he and Tom McCants had gone out on a
kangaroo hunt. Dorrie and her family were hunting kangaroos, too, and the two hunting parties joined forces. I
don't know how well Dorrie did at bagging kangaroos, but
she did a thorough job with Phil.

In observance of tradition, they were to have a banquet

instead of a reception after the wedding. On such occasions, the father of the bride customarily gets up and makes a talk, and is answered by the father of the groom. Phil asked me to act as stand-in for his father.

It was a beautiful wedding. We had all been away from home so long that we watched it with tears in our eyes, more like schoolgirls than fighting men. And afterward came the banquet.

The father of the bride, when his time came, got up and made a very nice talk and told a few jokes. Then he sat down and everybody looked at me.

I had what I thought was a wonderful joke to tell. It was about a boy who thought his pet turtle had died. To console him, his father promised such an elaborate funeral that when they discovered the turtle was still alive, the boy said, "Pop, let's kill him." So I got up full of confidence and began a long, elaborate version of the story, and at the first appropriate pause I looked at Phil to see how he was enjoying it.

He had turned ashy white, and his hands were shaking.

Bewildered, I looked at the other officers of the *Flasher*. The face of each of them mirrored some degree of discomfort, unease, or downright horror.

Badly shaken, I stumbled through the remainder of the story, and when it was over, the officers of the *Flasher*, the bridegroom included, almost broke up the banquet with their insane laughter. Not until they explained later did I understand the note of relief in their guffaws: they had thought that, on this most proper occasion, I was launching into an obscene story. When it turned out to be harmless, they were too delighted to care whether it was funny or not.

While Phil and Dorrie were gone on their honeymoon, the rest of us had another memorable rest at Perth and I got acquainted with my new boss. On December 30, Rear Admiral James Fife, Jr., had relieved Admiral Christie as Commander of Submarines, Southwest Pacific. He was a fine officer, with an intensity of devotion to command and a driving spirit. As the number of Japanese naval prizes afloat continued to dwindle, he would have the job of commanding the mop-up. He left no doubt there would be no letup in zeal at his headquarters in the days ahead.

The *Flasher* set out on its sixth war patrol on January 27, 1945. Phil was with us, a big photograph of Dorrie over his bunk, but Snap Coffin stayed behind to get his teeth fixed, denying hotly that he had ground them down to the nerves during his period as navigator. Eddie Atkinson, grim at the recent news of the death of his brother in action in India, moved up to Snap's place as engineering and diving officer, and Bob Harner, a young graduate of the Submarine School, took Eddie's place as commissary and assistant torpedo officer.

For all Admiral Fife's urgency of purpose, as we left this time our sights were frankly set on Mare Island. At the end of this run, we knew, we would go to Pearl Harbor and thence to the Navy Yard for a refit that would require at least two and a half months. We would all get thirty days' leave. It was a wonderful prospect, but at the same time it was demoralizing. I knew that whenever we went in for an attack, there would be an insidious voice in my consciousness saying, "Be careful. You're going home when this is over."

I was learning increasingly the loneliness of command. However small the unit, the CO is a little apart from the other officers. No matter how good they are or how friendly the skipper might be, there is still a reminder of the difference in responsibility when they say "Yes, sir," or in the way they call him "Captain." That is as it should be, but it leaves a man occasionally with an empty feeling.

Idleness accentuated it. Most of the days spent on a submarine patrol are uneventful, and the captain's insulation from routine makes time pass slowly. I went out of my way to be ingratiating to Phil, in order to get him to play cribbage with me instead of dreaming about Dorrie. But even Phil had more duties than I did, and boredom mounted as we moved toward our patrol area.

The days fell into a pattern for me. After we went through Lombok Strait — this time without incident — and were in enemy waters, I would leave word in the night order book to be called at five thirty, about half an hour before time for the daytime dive. The officer of the deck called me in the morning, I got up and climbed sleepily to the bridge to look around and talk, and finally, as reports continued to come up, he reported, "All right, we're ready to dive." I went down the hatch, saying, "Okay, take her down," and feeling a little useless as he sounded the diving alarm.

Then I went to the wardroom to eat breakfast and try to budget my day to avoid boredom. If it was a really quiet day, I went back to bed. The sleeping was better when we were submerged, because everything was secure and with a good man on the periscope I knew we wouldn't be surprised. After a couple of hours' sleep I got up, read awhile, worried about my tendency to eat too much candy and peanuts, wrote to Ann, and looked for a game of cribbage. Occasionally I would order a drill, but most of the *Flasher's* men were such old hands by now that it was hardly necessary.

I walked through the boat often, talking with the men, kidding with them a little, trying to keep the feel of the boat. I read *Lee's Lieutenants* and *Admiral of the Ocean Sea* and listened to Beethoven's Fifth on our hi-fi record player. There is a myth that submariners have regular calisthenics to keep in shape on patrol, but I believe any officer who tried to enforce a regimen of calisthenics on a submarine would be laughed off the boat. Certainly I never tried it.

There were four staterooms in the officers' quarters and a bunk that could be let down in the wardroom. We had nine officers, which made it two to a stateroom. Poor Eddie Atkinson had to share mine; the rooms are pitifully small, and it is obviously a disadvantage to share space with the captain.

Daytime was the most uneventful part of the twenty-four hour cycle. As it got dark, the officer of the deck sent down word that we were preparing to surface, and the boat seemed to come to life. The surfacing alarm sounded, high-pressure air was blown into the main ballast tanks, and as the roar sounded, the ship began to rise. When the depth gauge showed the top of the conning-tower hatch was out of the water, it was swung open. I went up on the bridge then, for that was the moment when something unexpected was most likely to happen.

During the day, the pressure inside the submerged boat builds up to two or three inches of mercury above the atmospheric pressure, because of small air leaks. When the hatch is opened, you have to stand back, because the pressure inside the sub rushes out with such force that it has been known to blow people out with it. So there would be the rush of air as the hatch opened, and after a pause the sound of the officer of the deck and the lookouts going up the ladder. Then, in more dignified manner, I followed. The engines started, and the blower, to blow the rest of the air out of the main ballast tanks, and one or two engines were put on battery charge while the remainder of the power kept us slowly patrolling, looking for whatever came along.

Strangely enough, there was always a period when all hands had to get used to the fresh air. When it first came in, it smelled awful. For hours we had been accustomed to air impregnated with cooking odors and other smells, and the fresh air was almost disgusting for a few minutes.

After we surfaced, the tone of the boat seemed to grow more festive. I sat in the wardroom with the off-duty officers, talking, playing chess, listening to a bit of music or to Tokyo Rose on the radio. And every time the course was changed or something was sighted or the weather altered, there was a messenger at my elbow to tell me about it. After the day's inactivity, it was a relief.

Our meals were always a treat, for food on a submarine

during the war was excellent, and it was only a plethora of good things that had led us to ride Eddie Atkinson about the meals on the previous patrol. We had a comparatively large cold-storage and icebox area, and it held the best of everything unless the patrol lasted longer than was expected. In that case, the fresh frozen meat might give out and the diet would get a little meager, but still above what the civilians were eating back in the States. We baked our own bread every night, and one of the captain's happiest privileges was to go back about five in the morning, when the baker was taking bread out of the oven, and sample it while it was hot. And we had a magic machine on board that produced ice cream, to be topped off by fresh frozen strawberries or specially preserved whipping cream.

The closest we ever came to a food crisis on the *Flasher* was once when, after being at sea for a month, we ran out of whipping cream. Despite that, we remained sternly on station and ate our strawberry shortcake straight.

It is strange, when you recall such a life, to hear people deplore the privations and terrors of submarining. "But to be cooped up down there under the water all the time, never knowing where you are!" they say. Well, we almost always knew where we were, and we were on surface more than we were submerged, and I have never yet seen a submariner suffer any phobias or complexes as a result of the space limitations.

The men spent a higher proportion of time in the sack than most sailors. That was one of the great luxuries aboard a submarine. The work might be long and hazardous when they were at battle stations, but during the days and weeks of routine patrolling they could do their jobs, stand their watches, and still have lots of time for sleep and diversion. They played cards in the crew's mess, which was the counterpart of the wardroom. Coffee was always available, there was room for six men each at the four tables, and the club was in session twenty-four hours a day.

On quiet nights, any man who wanted to go up on the bridge for a breath of fresh air was free to do so. All he had to do was go up in the conning tower, stick his head up the hatch, and say, "Permission to come on the bridge, sir?" The officer of the deck would say, "Come on." But very few of the men ever did it. They preferred to stay below. Aside from those who stood watches on the bridge, there were men on the *Flasher* who never saw the sky from the time they left on patrol until they got back to port.

We had a brief period of excitement early in this sixth patrol, joining with a number of other submarines in a search for two Japanese battleships that were known to be making the run from Saigon to the Empire, but we never sighted them. The *Flasher* had been teamed with the *Bashaw* in a two-sub wolfpack with me in command, and after the unproductive chase of the task force, we patrolled the area near Hainan Island. On February 21, we found our first targets. They were pathetically small.

When we first sighted them through the mist about mid-afternoon, they looked like two destroyer escorts, but after two hours of maneuvering to get in for a closer look they turned out to be sea trucks, wooden cargo ships. This late in the war, the Japanese had become so desperate for bottoms that they were using wooden ships powered with diesel engines — small affairs, usually no more than fifty tons, that would carry a few men and some oil in drums.

Still, after all the unproductive weeks we decided they were worth our torpedoes. There would be enough moonlight soon for a gun attack, and I wanted to give Hoke Simpson of the *Bashaw* a chance at action, too. So we let them pass, surfaced to follow them, and sent a message to Hoke.

Shortly after seven that night we had picked up both targets, but by then it was raining and visibility was too poor for a good gun attack. The *Bashaw* expressed a desire to shoot two torpedoes at the sea trucks, so I told Hoke to go ahead, and we tracked as he made his approach. It was a good job, and within an hour he fired, disintegrating one of the targets but missing the other. He suggested a gun attack on the other, and we closed the range to watch. But something went wrong with the *Bashaw's* deck gun. It wouldn't fire, so we took over the job and kept popping away with our four-inch gun until the target capsized. The keel was sticking out of the water as we nosed in among the bits of wreckage, and men were clustered on the keel. They were a long way from home, and the water was cold. I picked up my megaphone and yelled in my best instruction-book Japanese. "Come aboard, we won't hurt you." They only stared at us.

At last we began to back out, and as we did I noticed two men clinging to our bow and trying to climb aboard. I sent two of our men on deck with guns to bring them aboard as prisoners.

Our "prisoners," who were rushed below, shaved, reclothed, and chained to the stanchions, turned out to be terrified teen-agers. I decided to interrogate them, so I put on a khaki shirt and some insignia and sat at the head of the wardroom table and had them brought before me. It was a comic-opera interrogation, the two of them shaking with fright while I tried to look stern as I mouthed sounds from an English-Japanese dictionary. At last they calmed down enough to reveal that one of them could speak a little English, and after that it went more easily. They were Chinese, impressed into the Japanese Navy at Hong Kong and happy to get out of it. That was their story, and I was doubly inclined to believe it when I examined a wallet that had been taken from their clothes. It had a picture of a familiar-looking Oriental in it, and at first we all thought it must be the Japanese crown prince. But on second look we recognized him — the lad who played Charlie Chan's son in the movies.

In the days that followed, our prisoners got along famously with us, and vice versa. We called them Wing and Wong and put one in the forward torpedo room and one in the after torpedo room. I've never seen anything like the way they worked. They kept those rooms shining. The crew made pets of them, giving them trinkets and bits of clothing. Each of them acquired a pair of GI shoes, and their pride in them was unlimited. They wouldn't even take them off at night when they slept.

Four days later, the *Bashaw* reported contact with a small merchant ship escorted by a *chidori*-type patrol boat. We worked in ahead of the target and stood by for Hoke's attack. But the target took a major zig soon after he dived, and as it continued to steam away it became apparent

Hoke's attack had failed. The *Flasher* went to battle stations.

We went down to periscope depth — a full moon ruled out a surface attack — and watched the *chidori* go by. Then the freighter loomed up and we swung left for a stern shot, planning a spread of three torpedoes.

We guessed the range at nine hundred yards and fired the three fish. A minute passed without a sound: the first one must have missed. Another minute, and still nothing. Glumly I began to swing around for a bow shot, feeling there was little chance of hitting him now.

Then, at two minutes and twenty seconds, the first torpedo hit him — and then the second, and the third.

It was fantastic. We had made at least a thirteen-hundred-yard range error, we had failed to put the spread on the torpedoes, and yet we had hit that tiny target. The freighter simply disappeared, leaving nothing but a wet spot in the water, the *chidori* chugged around for a few minutes and then high-tailed it out of there, and I called Bob Harner, our new officer, over to my corner of the conning tower.

"Say, Bob."

"Yessir?"

"Bob, it ain't always that easy."

It was his first attack.

It was only a little freighter, and we had attacked only because it chanced to escape the *Bashaw*, and we had sunk it by the wildest accident. But its importance, as it turned out, was considerable. It was the difference between a successful patrol and a dry run for the *Flasher* on that trip out.

It put another star on the crew's combat pins and heightened morale all out of proportion to its importance. And, after the war ended and the submarine scores were compiled by the Joint Army-Navy Assessment Committee, it took on new significance. The freighter's scant 850 tons put the *Flasher*'s tonnage record for the entire war over the 100,-000 mark and gave us the highest score of all the submarines. Without the freighter, the *Rasher*'s score of 99,901 tons would have been top. It also brought our total of ships sunk to 21, putting us fourth behind the *Tautog*, Dick O'Kane's *Tang*, and the *Silversides*. As every submarine veteran knows, such scores are of scant value in assessing the real story of work done, but I was proud and gratified that Reuben Whitaker's fine record on the *Flasher*'s first four patrols had been supported.

We sank two sampans a few days later, in an action memorable to me only for a factor I have already mentioned — the eyes of one of the victims. After we thought the boat had been abandoned, we went in close to toss a last grenade into the deckhouse, and a man whose back was covered with blood jumped up from the sternsheets, took a wild look around, tumbled over the side, and began swimming toward a sailboat. We were very close to him, and for a moment my eyes met his. It was an experience I have tried to forget.

Late in February, as our patrol was about to end and everyone was increasingly impatient to head for Pearl, I made a horrible mistake. I sent a message to Admiral Fife telling him we would have to leave the area a couple of days early if we couldn't refuel in Subic Bay. Back came his an-

swer, telling me it would be a fine idea: we could refuel in
Subic and go out for two more weeks before returning to
Pearl. I could cheerfully have cut my own throat.

Our forces had taken Luzon by then, and Admiral Fife
himself was in the bay aboard a submarine tender. The only
pleasure I got from our five-day stay in Subic was a flight
down to Palawan to spend some time with an Army Air
Force group flying bombers across the China Sea to Indochina. It was an opportunity to see how the other guys
lived. And after all the tales I had heard of luxurious life
in the Air Force, it was a surprise to discover the rugged
way these men lived — in tents in the jungle, flying almost
every day, with the whole China Sea between them and
their targets. I was there as an observer, because by then
the submarines and planes were working more closely than
ever, exchanging information and backing one another up
in various ways. One day a pilot flew me over Manila for a
look at the destruction there. In *our* war, beneath the water,
we hadn't seen any lasting signs of the fighting. It was an
awesome sight.

We left Subic in a wolfpack of eight submarines. The
war had taken on a new phase as the Japanese suffered one
defeat after another, ashore and on the seas. By now their
fleet was almost gone, but they were still trying to haul
provisions up from Singapore and along the Malay Peninsula to the Empire in every conceivable sort of craft. There
were a few warships around Saigon, so our force of submarines patrolled close inshore to the north of it, looking
for anything that might come along.

We stayed on the surface night and day, sighting only a
few small craft and feeling quite cocky in our virtual own-

ership of the ocean. Giff Clemenson, an old *Skipjack* shipmate of mine, had command of the sub next in line to me. It was a measure of changed conditions in the last two or three months that he sent me a blinker signal one fine day: "I challenge you to a baseball game on the beach. You bring the beer."

The air was filled with our planes, and on several occasions we acted as control tower for them, relaying messages, helping them find one another, and chatting with them.

It lasted forever, and it was unproductive, and the relief when we were finally ordered to proceed to Pearl by way of Saipan was tremendous. But one disciplinary problem that had originated early in the patrol and grown constantly more serious remained to be solved. I chose the night we transited Bashi Channel, north of the Philippines, to lay down the law.

It so happened that all the officers and a majority of the men on the *Flasher* were addicted to chocolate ice cream, a flavor I could not abide, although I was passionately fond of almost any other kind. Every time we had ice cream, which was very often, it was chocolate. Every time I would turn to Bob Harner, our new commissary officer, and say, "Bob, I don't want to throw my rank around on this ship, but you know I don't like chocolate ice cream." Bob's eyebrows would go up and he would assume a look of hurt pride. "Honest, Captain, I told 'em to have vanilla tonight." Then I would grit my teeth and everyone would smile sympathetically and go on eating his chocolate ice cream.

The night we went through Bashi Channel, chocolate ice

cream was served as usual, and I turned to Page and said, "Go get that official envelope off my desk."

When he returned with it, I rapped for order. "Gentlemen, this is Ship's Order No. 3987B. The executive officer will read it."

They all looked a little quizzical; they were never sure when I was kidding. Phil opened the envelope and read:

"Ship's Order No. 3987B. Hereafter, the ratio of chocolate ice cream to all other flavors served on board the U.S.S. *Flasher* shall not exceed one in three. Signed under my hand and seal this thirtieth day of March 1945. G. W. Grider, Commanding Officer."

It worked. Thenceforth, the variety of ice-cream flavors served on the *Flasher* was heart-warming. But every time we had anything but chocolate, the officers in the wardroom would shake their heads and mutter bitterly about the Edict of Bashi Channel.

We stopped off at Saipan for a day to refuel and left in company with four other subs. We were in tight formation, about a thousand yards apart, and just as it got dark the evening we left, there was a sudden terrible explosion near one of the subs. I suppose a plane returning from a bombing mission had had to dump its bombs, but every sub in the formation decided a Japanese submarine was on the prowl. We scattered like a bunch of chickens, and started racing for Pearl.

The *Flasher*, I am proud to say, got there first.

14

Into the Barn

I HAD NOW MADE nine war patrols on four different submarines, and when the *Flasher* passed under the Golden Gate Bridge at San Francisco a few weeks later, I found myself utterly punch-drunk. My nerves were shot, my sleeping and eating habits more irregular than they had ever been, and I had begun slipping into long periods of lassitude more demoralizing than mere fatigue. San Francisco and Mom Chung helped bring me back to trim.

The *Flasher* went to Hunter's Point, a Navy installation at San Francisco, for refitting, and all our wives were waiting to meet us. Ann had moved to Palos Verdes by then, and she and Billy and I had a wonderful thirty days' leave there before returning to Hunter's Point, where we remained about three months while work proceeded on the *Flasher*. We lived in a Quonset hut that probably would look small and bare to me now, but then it was heaven on earth. And while we were there, we met Mom.

Dr. Margaret Chung was a remarkable character, an American citizen of Chinese extraction and one of the most lovable ladies I have ever met. Even before the war began, she had "adopted" some aviators who were about to join the Dutch in Indonesia. They went to her for treatment of a skin disease, but before long she had moved them all into her house.

One day, one of them said, "Gee, Mom, I wish you could be our mother."

"I can't be your mother, because I'm not married," Mom told him, "but you can all be my fair-haired bastards."

That was the beginning of something that was a major contribution to the war effort in San Francisco. After the United States got into the war, the "bastards" joined our forces, and they would return to San Francisco occasionally and take other people around to meet Mom. She had a commodious house on Masonic Street, a heart as big as all outdoors, and lots of friends. She would take these boys in and feed them; they would bring their friends; and it became a custom that every Sunday night Mom had open house for her fair-haired bastards. She would "adopt" them and give them little symbols showing they belonged to the family. One night an aviator made the mistake of taking along a submariner, who persuaded Mom that she ought to extend her affection to the undersea branch. By the time I reached Hunter's Point, Mom was a tradition in the Submarine Service.

There would be easily a hundred people at her house on Sunday nights. Civilian friends all over San Francisco helped her. These "kiwis," as she called them, did everything from sharing the cost of the affairs to serving the food. Mom had a way of collecting important people for her gatherings. The first time Ann and I went to her house, Lily Pons was singing, Admiral Nimitz was dishing out the chow, and Harold Stassen was among his assistants. She called the submariners her Golden Dolphins. I still have my membership card, and we still hear from Mom now and then.

Once she took Ann and me and a few of her kiwi friends out for the evening. It was like being with the President of the United States. She would drive up to a night club, stop in the middle of the street, and get out, leaving the car for somebody to take care of. If the floor show was going on, they would stop it until Mom's party was seated. It was a very large evening.

But there was a somber undercurrent beneath the pleasures of our stay in San Francisco. A gadget was being put on the *Flasher* the purpose of which was to enable us to go through mine fields. We were to go into the Sea of Japan on our next patrol, to sink ships off the home shores of the Empire, and the new equipment was intended to make the job a little less hazardous. As the summer of 1945 approached and the war news grew daily more encouraging, all of us looked forward to this assignment with something less than enthusiasm.

We got back to Pearl in August and began a period of intensive training. Every day we went out and practiced traversing a dummy mine field. Every night we went into drydock so the snarled mine cables could be cut off our propellers. It was a little unnerving.

A day or two before we were scheduled to leave for the Empire, rumors began to hit the newspapers that the Japanese were about to surrender, and the very night before we were to leave, the news became official. Pearl Harbor was bedlam that night. Every ship in the harbor was firing guns into the air, and every admiral in Hawaii was sending out dispatches telling us all to stop it. I have always believed the *Flasher* sent out the most impressive display of all. We used our entire supply of recognition signals, firing them from a little mortar on the bridge. We fired one a second. They all had parachutes on them, and they were a beautiful sight, floating down toward the water, each of them a different color. I invited all the old chiefs to the wardroom and broke out the ship's supply of brandy — that same variety of brandy that had tasted so awful to Roger Paine and me so long ago — and each of us took a little two-ounce bottle, poured it in a glass, and drank a toast to the peace.

The celebration continued for three or four days. I remember the next night I went out to see some friends who lived in the Waikiki district of Honolulu. There was to be a party, so I had gone by the Royal Hawaiian first and acquired about fifty steaks. I reached the apartment with them, all right, and there were at least fifty people there already. There would have been plenty of steaks except for what happened next. We heard a noise outdoors and went out to look. A parade was coming down the street, somehow its members got confused with our party, and the whole parade ended up in that one little apartment. It was a madhouse.

A group of subs went back to the States almost immediately, and after the second day we on the *Flasher* stayed close aboard, hoping for our orders and watching the other subs depart. By some spontaneous instinct, as the first one backed out of the slip at the submarine base and turned to head out, every man aboard threw his hat over the side, and after that every other sub followed suit. They all had happy slogans on their periscope shears, and as they disappeared into the east we grinned at each other and speculated on how soon we would follow.

It was a week before our orders came. They directed us to Guam.

We could hardly believe it. Four subs, the *Flasher* among them, had been ordered to some vague duty in the Mariannas.

We backed out of the base in a bitterness of spirit that extended from the captain to the mess boy. No hats hit the water, and no signs waved from our periscope shears.

For a day and half a night we proceeded toward Guam. Then we picked up a code message addressed to the officer in tactical command of the formation. The *Flasher* had a very sharp team of decoders, and they had the message translated before the commander did. They came up the hatch like an explosion to tell me the news.

"Captain! We've been ordered back to Pearl!"

I took one look at the message, turned the *Flasher* around, and gave the order for top speed: "Full ahead Pearl!"

From another sub the formation commander noted that we had dropped out of formation and sent me a blinker signal.

"Where are you going?" it said.

"You'll know in a minute," I messaged. We beat the group back to Pearl that time, too.

We were in Pearl only a few days before orders came to proceed to New London, Connecticut. It was into the barn at last for the gallant *Flasher*.

The trip from Pearl Harbor to Panama is one of the longest overseas voyages you can make, and we enjoyed every moment of it. The weather was beautiful, the outlook was sunny, even the ocean seemed friendly. I don't believe we dived a single time. Our only encounter was with a whale.

A couple of days out of Panama, we ran into what must have been a meadowland, an area very productive of vegetable matter, and it was teeming with all kinds of fish. I had seen a lot of porpoises during my Navy career, but never the number we saw that day. There must have been ten thousand of them, leaping all over the water. There were schools of tuna everywhere. And suddenly, as we were headed southeast, we sighted two whales broad on the starboard bow, headed northeast, on a steady course and speed, at a range of about five miles.

I changed course a little, just to get close enough to see them. We held course and speed, and so did they. Finally, when we got about half a mile away, I turned to the officer of the deck.

"Well," I said, "maybe we ought to slow down. They've got the right of way."

We slowed a little, and stood there waiting for them to sound or turn when they saw us. But they didn't. Finally I had to order all back emergency, and even then we bumped one of them with the bow.

They both went down after that. It was a light blow, and I don't believe we hurt the whale. We decided they were both asleep until the collision roused them. But asleep or not, they were making about ten knots.

At Panama, another change in orders awaited us. We were to go first to New Orleans. So we proceeded up the Gulf, cocky as the Lord, feeling that we had won the war and inherited the universe. When we got to the mouth of the Mississippi, we were asked if we needed a pilot. "Hell, no," we messaged back. "We can navigate this river all by ourselves."

We entered it at night, and that night was a real nightmare. The river was only a few inches lower than the bank, we couldn't see any landmarks, and no one aboard knew the rules of the road for the Mississippi. Every time we passed a steamer we almost collided, and once we came within inches of cutting a dredge pipe in two. Finally, after a sleepless night, we reached New Orleans, where it developed we couldn't find the supply depot. We moved along like a carload of lost vacationers, shouting questions to everyone we saw on the piers, until finally we located it. Later, one of the *Flasher* officers had a date with the daughter of a river pilot and came back with word that we were the first deep-draft ship that had come up without a pilot in a generation. I don't know whether that is accurate or not, but I am sure of one thing: I'd never try it again.

The *Flasher* stayed in New Orleans two or three months, doing nothing, while Ann and I had another memorable vacation, and then we were ordered to Mobile for Navy Day. From there we were to go to Philadelphia for decommission.

Since we would be in Mobile for the first Navy Day

after the war, it seemed only fitting that the job be done properly. A new officer, Hank Drumwright, had joined the *Flasher* at Hunter's Point and had demonstrated his resourcefulness many times; I sent him ahead to prepare the way for us and make whatever arrangements were necessary to assure that our part in the celebration would be memorable. Hank really outdid himself. It turned out that a cruiser, an aircraft carrier, and two submarines had been ordered to Mobile for the day, but our advance man had whitewashed them all. We led the parades, the parties were in our honor, and the newspapers were full of the *Flasher*. It was downright embarrassing, especially when I was called on to make a speech. Back at the Naval Academy, I had memorized a speech for just such an occasion, one based on a great naval commander of the past. But it was my misfortune to have chosen Admiral Farragut, the Union hero of Mobile Bay.

My friend Sam Nickey came down from Memphis, and I invited him to ride on the *Flasher* with us to Key West. It was against regulations, but I knew no one would be checking too closely, and I wanted to even the score with Sam for various practical jokes he had played on me in the past. One day he wandered to the afterpart of the bridge, a good twenty-five feet from the hatch, and I waited until his back was turned and then sounded the diving alarm. It didn't work, though. Sam was the first man down the hatch.

From Key West we went to Philadelphia, where we stayed a few months more before our battery was removed and we were ignominiously towed to New London, where the *Flasher* went into mothballs. There were only a few of the crew left with us by then, and about three officers. During the brief decommissioning ceremony we stood and looked at that old hulk that had taken us through so much, and there wasn't a dry eye among us. Nothing memorable was said; we simply read the orders and hauled down the commission pennant, and they gave me a pen and pencil set; but it was one of the memorable moments of my life. All I could do was choke up and say "Thanks."

I was ordered back to Key West then, to take command of the U.S.S. *Cubera*, a brand-new submarine. I was back in the peacetime Navy. And now we needed a larger house than before, because besides Ann and Billy there was Gail. Since early in the war, Ann had been carrying on a long campaign to find a child we could adopt. It was extremely difficult in those days for people in the service to adopt children, but Ann's hard work had paid off at last, and while we were in Philadelphia our beautiful three-year-old daughter arrived. It was a great thrill, and more than that, for Ann had broken the ice for other couples in the Submarine Service. In the years since then, twenty-five or thirty submariners have adopted babies through the same agency that gave us Gail.

War leaves many loose threads, but two of them were gathered up when we arrived at Key West. The man I was to succeed as captain of the *Cubera* was Roger Paine, my earliest friend aboard the *Wahoo*, who was now going off to become an expert on atomic warfare. And Jack Griggs, also of the *Wahoo*, was my engineering officer.

I had the *Cubera* for about a year, a happy, peaceful time during which we adopted another child, Sally, and began to see other friends get the children they had longed for. Operating conditions at the submarine base were ideal, the work we were doing was interesting, and the *Cubera* was a fine ship. I worried a little over what seemed to me to be indications that the Navy was slipping back into some of its former peacetime errors — growing supercautious, renewing some of the discarded routines and red tape we would have been better off without — but I suppose that happened to all combat veterans when they settled down to a peacetime routine. On the whole, I was happy with life and in love with my naval career when, just as the *Cubera* came into dock one afternoon, I felt a strange pain in my chest, radiating out into my arms and up into my neck. It was not terribly painful, but it was unusual and very uncomfortable.

The lady who had helped us adopt our children was in Key West that day, and we were having a lawn party for her and four submarine families who had also adopted children. I was expected at the party, but I went first to the dispensary. A young doctor there looked me over, said it sounded to him like a heart attack, and advised that I go to the hospital.

He sounded fairly calm about it, though, so I decided he was only humoring me. I went to the lawn party instead, and after a while the pain disappeared. It returned briefly that night, just enough to make me go to the hospital the next day. The doctor thumped me and tested me and said it wasn't likely a heart attack at my age — I was thirty-five then — but that it wouldn't hurt to be sure. The man who operated the electrocardiograph was on leave, he said, but he'd be back in ten days and maybe I'd better return then. So I went back to my normal routine, operating the *Cubera* during the week and playing center field on the softball team on week ends, and almost forgot it. One day I remembered and sauntered over to the hospital for a test.

Something went wrong with the first print, so they took another. It was even worse. When the doctor looked at it, he seemed worried, and for the first time I felt a cold, sinking sensation. But after the third test, the operator came back with the developed film, and his face was wreathed in smiles.

"This one's perfect!" he told the doctor. "It came out beautifully!"

I grinned at him. "Thank God. I was getting worried."

He looked at me curiously over the print. "Oh, it looks like you've had a heart attack, all right. But it's a beautiful print."

The doctor grabbed the print, looked at it, and told me I did indeed have a serious heart condition. He rushed me to bed, cautioned me that any excitement or activity might be fatal, warned me not to worry, and left me. I was a quivering bowl of jelly by morning.

I lay in the hospital bed for two or three weeks, gradually getting my sense of perspective back, and finally asked the doctor when the most dangerous period was. He said it was immediately after the attack itself. Recalling that I had had an unusually good day in center field only a few days after the attack, I felt sufficiently reassured to ask another question: "Who is the best heart specialist in the world?"

"Dr. Paul Dudley White," he told me promptly. "In Boston."

"Then I want sick leave," I said.

They gave it to me, and I wrote Dr. White a special-delivery airmail letter telling him I was coming and then left before he had time to reply. I bummed my way up by various Navy flights to Boston, stopping in New London en route to visit Chester Nimitz, Jr., and his wife Joan. I thought it might be the last time I would ever see them.

As I hobbled into their living room, Chester grabbed my hand, shook it vigorously, and announced we would all go swimming in honor of my arrival. I told him I couldn't. He dug around in a drawer and threw me a pair of trunks. "Aw, hell," he said. "Put 'em on."

I did, filled with misgivings, and walked timidly down to the water to watch Chester and Joan swim.

"Come on in, you coward!" he yelled.

"Chester, I've just had a heart attack. I'm afraid if I do, it'll kill me."

He snorted. "Well, for Christ's sake, jump in and find out."

It may have been the beginning of my recovery. I did jump in, and it didn't kill me, and I began to think I might survive after all.

Dr. White did more to convince me. He made me walk up a flight of stairs with him, an undertaking that in my frame of mind was like scaling Mount Everest, and he assured me that if my attack had been more than a mild one, I would probably have been dead long before I got to Boston.

Hesitantly, I began to ask what I could do. Play golf? "Yes." Tennis? "Sure." Handball? "Certainly." Ski? "Fine, good for you." I began naming every sport I could think of. When I got to football, he held up his hand. "At your age," he said, "you ought to quit about the end of the third quarter."

I suppose it was a sort of psychological shock treatment, and it did wonders for me. It was like a reprieve from a living death. I am not the quiet, reflective type, and I had become convinced at Key West that my future, such as it was, lay in complete inactivity.

Dr. White wrote a letter outlining my condition, and I went back to Key West with it and spent a couple of months on sick leave, swimming daily in the officers' club pool while the younger Navy doctors stood on the side and exchanged bets on how soon I would float to the top, belly first. Then I went before the retiring board. They asked if I wanted to get out, and I said yes. With that heart attack on my record, I was convinced my opportunities for advancement in the Navy would be increasingly limited.

While the *Flasher* was at Philadelphia, I had run into an old Naval Academy classmate who was about to be court-martialed because of an accident involving his ship. We discussed the legal aspects of the trial at great length, and when I learned subsequently that it had come out just as I had predicted — he had been tried and convicted, but the conviction was reversed by the Judge Advocate General's office — I decided the law was a fascinating field. Now, as I waited for my separation from the service, I recalled that and wondered if it was too late for me to become a lawyer. It is hard to plan a new career from the very beginning after years in something else.

One day an old friend of mine from Memphis, John Apperson, came to see me at Key West. We talked about the future. "Study law and come in with us," John said. "I'll give you an office overlooking the Mississippi River."

So Ann and the children and I moved to Charlottesville, and I went to law school at the University of Virginia. We returned to Memphis with my law degree and another child, Wilson, and I moved into the office overlooking the river. Since then I have joined another firm, and the view of the river is gone. But a hard law case or a tight political campaign, I have learned, bears much in common with an attack on a convoy. The long, painful approach to the problem, the delicate maneuvering for position, the hard moments of doubt and indecision, and finally the committal of all your forces in the move that must eventually mean success or failure – the outline is the same. When I left submarines, I wondered if I would ever find enough action to make me happy. Now I sometimes find myself thinking of the good old days when I could relax and take it easy.

15

The Last of the Corsairs

EVEN BEFORE I LEFT the Navy, major changes in submarine design had begun to appear and revolutionary changes were being talked about. The *Cubera* was already scheduled for a major overhaul, to emerge as a guppy-type submarine with a snorkel. Her deck would be cleared of guns, which had proved during the war to be of only minor value, and any other clutter that would cut down her speed. Her superstructure and conning tower would be streamlined, and the snorkel, a device perfected by Germany late in the war, would be installed. The snorkel allows diesel-driven submarines an opportunity to breathe without coming to the surface. A tube rising above the bridge makes it possible for air to be sucked in from the surface while the submarine is at periscope depth. Without the snorkel, diesels could not be used under water because of their need for air, and whenever we had to run the diesels to recharge our batteries, we had to surface. With the snorkel, a submarine need rise no higher than periscope depth for weeks at a time.

But this was only the beginning. Already, as I took my leave of Key West, the world's first true submarine was being planned: this time no surface boat capable of submersing for limited periods, but a craft that could run under water indefinitely. The arrival of the atomic age had made possible a power plant that required no air, and the building of the nuclear-powered *Nautilus* would shortly make the submarine Jules Verne dreamed of a reality: a craft that could travel twenty thousand leagues or more without refueling, that could run under the polar icecap or circle the world without surfacing; a new type of war fish that, as the submariners soon began saying, would have to come to the surface only every four years to let the crew re-enlist.

For a generation whose eyes have been more in the air than on the sea, it is hard to realize the staggering advances that have been made in submarine design within a few years. Actually, as an effective tool of naval warfare, the submarine is only a phenomenon of the twentieth century. It was used as early as the Revolutionary War, when a one-man submersible, the *Turtle,* tried and failed to sink a British man-of-war anchored off Governors Island at New York. But, while inventors continued to work through the years on better submarines, the nations of the world virtually ignored their possibilities, and the larger naval powers were actually hostile to them, seeing in them only a weapon for the inferior powers. Robert Fulton could find no support for his own *Nautilus* either at home or abroad. Not until the Civil War, when the hand-propelled Confederate submersible, the *Hunley,* sank the sloop-of-war U.S.S. *Housatonic* off Charleston and was itself lost, with all nine crew members, in the operation, did a submarine destroy its first enemy vessel. The United States Navy did not acquire its first submarine until 1900, and the *Hunley*'s feat remained unduplicated until World War I.

Now, almost overnight, the submarine has come into its own and assumed an increasingly important role in the fleet plans of all the major nations. Its potentialities as a launcher of guided missiles are recognized as tremendous; as early as 1947, a missile was fired from the deck of a submarine off Point Mogu, California. Torpedoes with new and fabulous properties, such as the sound-guided homing torpedo and the pattern-running torpedo, have multiplied the submarine's effectiveness as a weapon against surface craft. The use of subs as troop carriers, oilers, mine layers, and radar picket boats is increasing. New attack subs built since the war — inclu g namesakes of the sunken *Wahoo* and *Tang* — can run faster submerged than on the surface, a direct reversal of the situation that made approaches on distant convoys so difficult during the war. The *Skipjack*, the first submarine I ever served on, was the newest and best in the fleet at the time I joined her, less than two years before Pearl Harbor. Today she is obsolete, and as this is written a new nuclear-powered *Skipjack* is under construction, expected to be the fastest and most maneuverable sub in the world when she is completed.

Where the revolutionary changes in submarine design will lead no one can yet be sure. The growing talk of the all-submersible navy of the future, in which even battleships and aircraft carriers can submerge for greater safety or secrecy, may or may not be a pipe dream. But on one point there can be no doubt: the submarine has proved its right to an increasingly major share of naval planning.

For a submariner it is a great prospect, a confirmation of the faith all submariners have in their boats, a demonstration at last that the sub is not the strange, outlandish freak it was once considered, but an instrument in the main stream of naval development. But for a romantic, there is a touch of regret in these great strides, just as there must have been for the air aces of World War I who saw the airplane grow into something so vast that individual personalities were lost.

We were corsairs in the Pacific conflict, and I believe we were the last of the corsairs. For a while we wore the mantle of the old corsairs of generations past. We were granted what may have been the last taste of individuality in modern warfare. War has been hell through the centuries, but until the single unit was lost in the masses of groups, squadrons, fleets, and army corps there was still something bearable about it, an opportunity to see the conflict in personal terms, a chance to hang on to some shred of romance in a sea of hatred. When you think of yourself as a lone wolf stalking the seas, searching down the enemy and engaging him in personal combat, it is a thing you can grasp. It is man-sized rather than incredibly colossal; an element of sanity remains.

The cavalry had it in the Civil War, this feeling that the individual still amounted to something. The war birds, my father among them, had it in World War I. And we in the Submarine Service had it during those grim years in the Pacific. But the submarine of the future will be too big, too important, too thoroughly integrated into over-all strategy, for corsairs. In its preatomic form, it was almost an anachronism, a nineteenth-century weapon that developed late and thereby brought into the twentieth century a last taste of what made warfare bearable in other generations. In a world of nuclear physics, it is unlikely that any new element of romance, whether by land or sea or air, will temper the wars of the future.

We were the last of the corsairs. It is a conviction that has grown in me since those final months in the Pacific, and it is a conviction that leaves me with mixed emotions: gratitude, and some pride, and much nostalgia — and, as I look at my sons and think of the future, a cold sense of foreboding.

Date Due

MAY 3 '60			
MAR 30 '63			
APR 9 '6?			
APR 1 '64			
APR 15 '64			
MAY 11 '64			
OCT 23 '64			
APR 7 '65			
APR 12 '65			
JUN 21 '67			
NOV 15 '68			
MAR 19 '69			
APR 2 '69			
NOV 13 '69			
MR 2 '77			
FE 17 '81			
𝒢𝒷	PRINTED	IN U. S. A.	